Henry Lake Gilmour, William J. Kirkpatrick

Gospel Praises for Use in Meetings of Christian Worship

Henry Lake Gilmour, William J. Kirkpatrick

Gospel Praises for Use in Meetings of Christian Worship

ISBN/EAN: 9783337290085

Printed in Europe, USA, Canada, Australia, Japan

Cover: Foto ©Lupo / pixelio.de

More available books at **www.hansebooks.com**

Gospel Praises

FOR USE IN

MEETINGS OF CHRISTIAN

WORSHIP.

EDITED BY

WM. J. KIRKPATRICK,   H. L. GILMOUR,
J. LINCOLN HALL,

HALL-MACK CO.,
Publishers,
1020 ARCH ST., PHILADELPHIA.

Single copy, 30c.   Per hundred, $25.

PREFACE.

GOSPEL PRAISES contains over 150 new pieces; also a collection of over 100 standard gospel songs which have made a place for themselves in the hearts of Christian people.

In no book heretofore published will be found so great and varied a selection as is to be found in GOSPEL PRAISES.

Every department of Christian worship, whether it be the Gospel Meeting, the Young People's Society, or the Sunday School, is given a great number of songs in this book,

All that is best in the field of religious hymns will be found in GOSPEL PRAISES.

THE EDITORS.

THE TEN COMMANDMENTS.

1. Thou shalt have no other gods before me.

2. Thou shalt not make unto thee any graven image, or any likeness of *any thing* that *is* in heaven above, or that *is* in the earth beneath, or that *is* in the water under the earth: thou shalt not bow down thyself to them, nor serve them: for I the Lord thy God *am* a jealous God, visiting the iniquity of the fathers upon the children unto the third and fourth *generation* of them that hate me; and showing mercy unto thousands of them that love me, and keep my commandments.

3. Thou shalt not take the name of the Lord thy God in vain: for the Lord will not hold him guiltless that taketh his name in vain.

4. Remember the Sabbath day, to keep it holy. Six days shalt thou labor, and do all thy work: but the seventh day *is* the Sabbath of the Lord thy God: *in it* thou shalt not do any work, thou, nor thy son, nor thy daughter, thy manservant, nor thy maidservant, nor thy cattle, nor thy stranger that *is* within thy gates: for *in* six days the Lord made heaven and earth, the sea, and all that in them *is*, and rested the seventh day: wherefore the Lord blessed the Sabbath day, and hallowed it.

5. Honor thy father and thy mother: that thy days may be long upon the land which the Lord thy God giveth thee.

6. Thou shalt not kill.

7. Thou shalt not commit adultery.

8. Thou shalt not steal.

9. Thou shalt not bear false witness against thy neighbor.

10. Thou shalt not covet thy neighbor's house, thou shalt not covet thy neighbor's wife, nor his manservant, nor his maidservant, nor his ox, nor his ass, nor anything that *is* thy neighbor's.—Ex. 20: 3-17.

THE APOSTLES' CREED.

I believe in God the Father Almighty, Maker of heaven and earth. And in Jesus Christ his only begotten Son our Lord: who was conceived by the Holy Ghost, born of the Virgin Mary; suffered under Pontius Pilate, was crucified, dead and buried; he descended into hades; the third day he rose from the dead; he ascended into heaven; and sitteth at the right hand of God the Father Almighty; from thence he shall come to judge the quick and the dead. I believe in the Holy Ghost; the holy catholic Church, the communion of saints, the forgiveness of sins; the resurrection of the body, and the life everlasting. Amen.

OLD HUNDRED. L. M.

THOMAS KEN. GUILLAUME FRANC.

Praise God, from whom all blessings flow, Praise him, all creatures here below;

Praise him a-bove, ye heavenly host; Praise Father, Son, and Ho-ly Ghost!

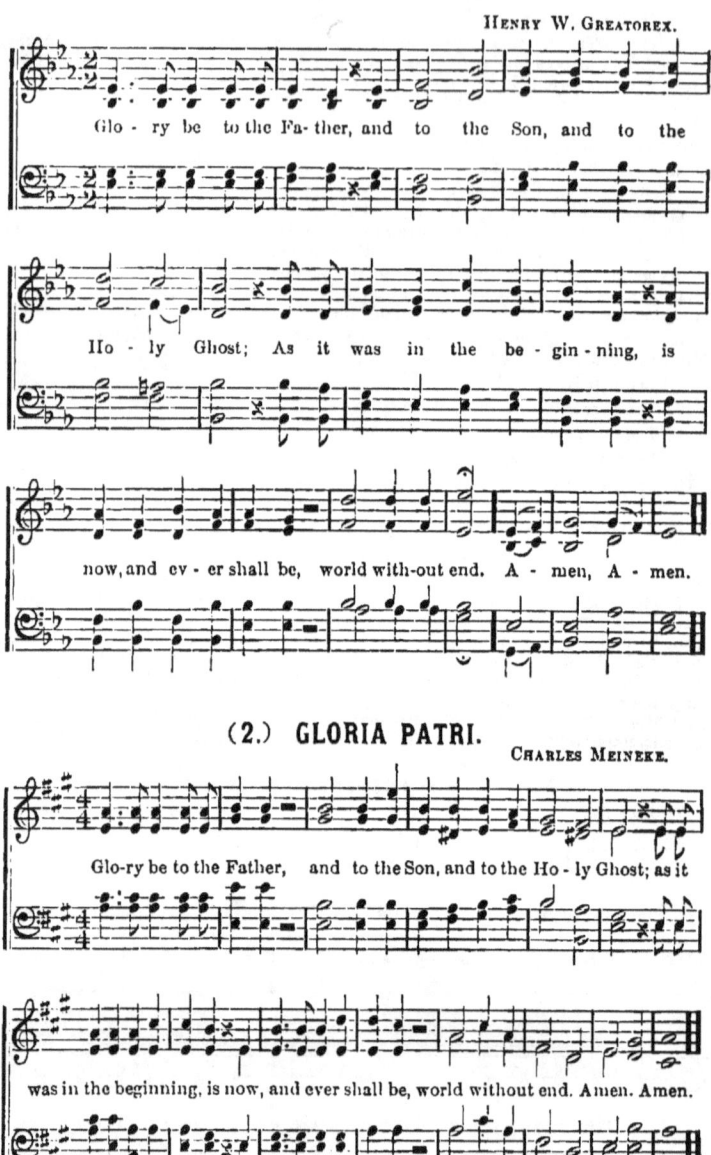

PROMISES OF JESUS.

A. A. PAYN.
C. AUSTIN MILES.

1. Promis-es of Jesus! How they cheer the heart Of the fainting Christian,
2. For each precious promise Jesus Christ has made Will be kept in fullness,
3. Tho' upon the earth his form no more we see, Words that he has spoken
4. When he comes again, to meet the faithful here Who a-wait his presence,

and new life impart To the wea-ry trav'ler on the upward road; And
though it seem delayed; We in faith behold-ing rich-es in his Word Will
ne'er for-got shall be; Hear the Saviour's message, and believe 'tis true, "I
and with heart sincere Long for his appear-ing, may he bid us come And

CHORUS.

how they help to light-en ev-'ry load.
sing again his praise with one accord.
go, and I'll prepare a place for you."
dwell with him in our e-ter-nal home.

Ho-san-na! ho-san-na! to

Jesus Christ, our King! Hosanna! hosanna! his praises let us sing; For blessing which he

gives us in promises so sure—Tho' heav'n and earth may pass away, they shall endure.

Copyright, 1899, by Hall-Mack Co.

PARDONED AND FREE.

J. W. V. J. W. VanDeVenter.

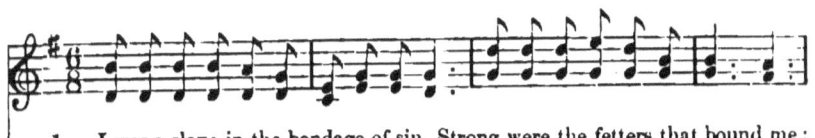

1. I was a slave in the bondage of sin, Strong were the fetters that bound me;
2. Sad was my life, when in darkness and doubt I was forlorn and forsak-en,
3. Now I rejoice in his favor and care, Comfort and friends are surrounding;
4. How can I pay him for saving my soul? How can I live for his glo - ry?

Now I am free, for the Lord took me in, Jesus the Saviour hath found me.
Till the dear Saviour in love brought me out, Then were my fetters all taken.
I am no longer in sin and despair, Wonderful love is a- bound- ing.
I can tell others how Christ made me whole, Tell the most wonderful sto- ry.

CHORUS.

Free, free, pardoned and free, Je- sus hath found me and spok - en;

Free, free, pardoned and free, All of my chains have been bro - ken.

"ALL THE DAY LONG."

"All the day long have I stretched forth my hand unto a disobedient and gainsaying people."—Rom. 10: 21.

Rev. W. B. Williams.   Dedicated to Mrs. J. G. Wilson.   H. L. Gilmour.

(SOLO OR DUET AD LIB. AND CHORUS.)

1. "All the day long I have stretched forth my hands," While mercy-drops fall from the
2. All the day long ye have heard my voice call Up-on you to come un-to
3. All the day long hath my Spir-it been true, In showing your soul its vile
4. All the day long! but soon this will end! Then cometh the day of your

tip of each finger; And all the day long ye have spurned my demands, Pre-
me and sur-render; And all the day long do my earnest pleas fall In
sin and transgression; And all the day long have I found yet in you No
judgment and sorrow! O turn un-to me, on my mer-cy de-pend, Re-

Chorus.

ferring in guilt and in darkness to lin-ger.
vain on your ears, no mat-ter how ten-der.
signs of re-gret, nor an-y con-fes-sion.
pent and be saved before dawneth the morrow.

"Come unto me, all ye that

ritard............

labor and are heavy laden, And I will give you rest, I will give you rest."

Copyright, 1899, by H. L. Gilmour, Wenonah, N. J.

STRENGTH FOR MY DAY.

"And as thy days, so shall thy strength be."

Mrs. Mary B. Wingate.   H. L. Gilmour.

1. There's strength for my day, and whatever may come I'll cling to the promise divine; Thro' fast falling tears, and thro' heartaches and fears, I claim the sweet message as mine.
2. There's strength for my day, and I'm needing it so, There's light in the darkness to shine; It comforts me so while re-peating it o'er, I claim the sweet message as mine.
3. There's strength for my day, and why should I despair, Why longer in loneliness pine? A Help-er is near and a Friend that is dear, I claim the sweet message as mine.
4. There's strength for my day, and what more can I ask When reading this promise divine? Tho' doubts may distress, and tho' cares may oppress, I claim the sweet message as mine.

CHORUS. (Psalm 84: 11.)

"For the Lord God is a sun and shield: the Lord will give grace and glory: no good thing will he withhold from them that walk uprightly."

Copyright, 1899, by H. L. Gilmour, Wenonah, N. J.

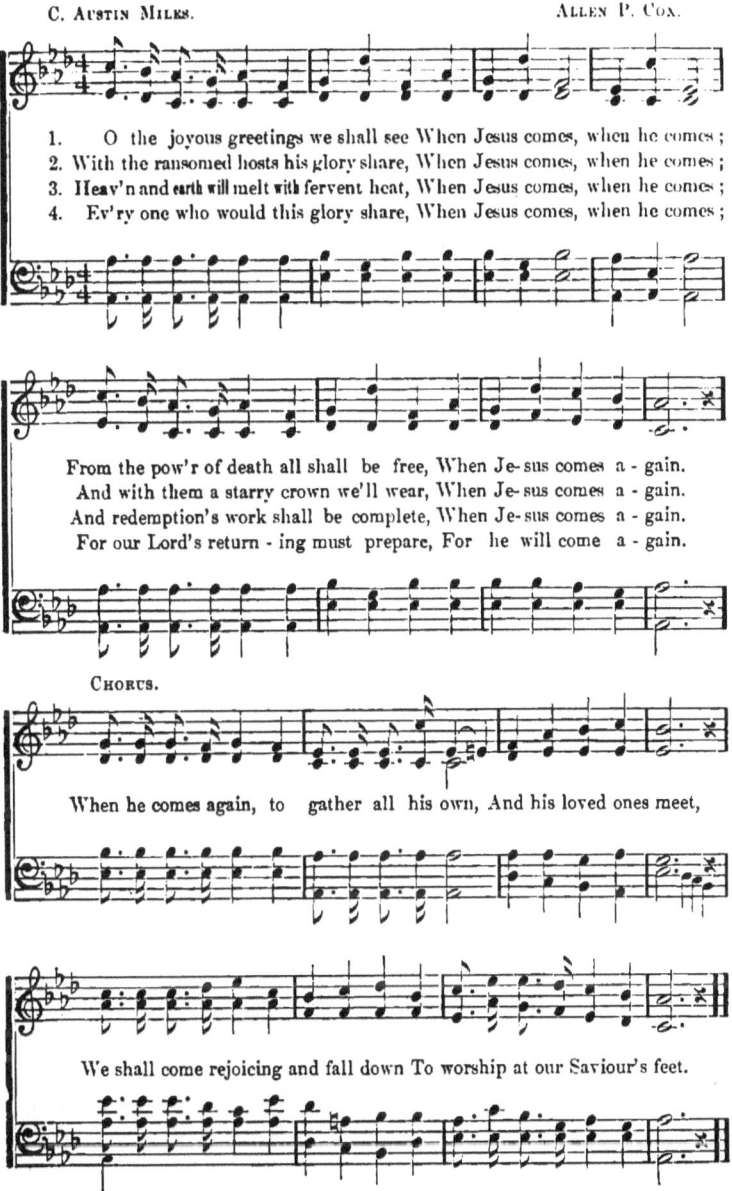

HIS WAY WITH THEE.

C. S. N. Psalm 37: 5. Rev. Cyrus S. Nusbaum.
(Consecration.)

1. Would you live for Jesus, and be always pure and good? Would you walk with
2. Would you have him make you free, and follow at his call? Would you know the
3. Would you in his kingdom find a place of constant rest? Would you prove him

him with-in the nar-row road? Would you have him bear your burden,
peace that comes by giv-ing all? Would you have him save you, so that
true each prov-i-den-tial test? Would you in his ser-vice la-bor

Chorus.

carry all your load? Let him have his way with thee.
you need never fall? Let him have his way with thee. } His power can make you what you
always at your best? Let him have his way with thee.

ought to be; His blood can cleanse your heart and make you free; His love can

rit.

fill your soul, and you will see 'Twas best for him to have his way with thee.

Copyright, 1899, by H. L. Gilmour, Wenonah, N. J.

HEREAFTER.

19

E. E. Hewitt.
Geo. H. Hewitt.

1. Yes, here-af-ter, we shall know Why these tears of sor-row flow,
2. Let us trust to his dear hand, All we can-not un-der-stand;
3. Je-sus notes the se-cret sigh, Hears the fer-vent, hum-ble cry;
4. Then we'll leave it all with him; Earth-ly shad-ows, strange and dim,

Find-ing ev-er-last-ing gain For the transient loss and pain.
Bright re-vealings he will show When, here-af-ter, we shall know.
Counts the heav-y steps, and slow, Whispers, "Wait and you shall know."
Van-ish all, in heaven's glow; There, here-af-ter, we shall know.

CHORUS.

In the land where Je-sus dwells, Where the sweet-est mu-sic swells,

We shall know, O we shall know, Why these tears of sor-row flow.

Copyright, 1899, by H. L. Gilmour, Wenonah, N. J.

I NEVER WILL LEAVE MY SAVIOUR.

Rev. Johnson Oatman, Jr. A. A. Baldwin.

1. Tho' in this world of sin and woe, I never will leave my Saviour;
2. Let friends prove false, let friends prove true, I never will leave my Saviour;
3. Tho' worldly pleasure bids me stay, I never will leave my Saviour;
4. Let fears ap-pall, let doubts as-sail, I never will leave my Saviour;

Tho' stormy winds around may blow, I nev-er will leave my Sav-iour.
No mat-ter what I may pass thro', I nev-er will leave my Sav-iour.
From all its smiles I'll turn a-way, I nev-er will leave my Sav-iour.
My anchor holds with-in the veil, I nev-er will leave my Sav-iour.

CHORUS.

I nev-er will leave my Saviour, I nev-er will leave my Saviour;

On Cal-va-ry he ransomed me, My precious, precious Sav-iour.

Copyright, 1899, by Wm. J. Kirkpatrick.

22 LIVING IN THE SUNSHINE.

"The path of the righteous is as the light of dawn, that shineth more and more unto the perfect day."—Prov. 4: 18 (R. V. margin).

S. H. B.   S. H. Bolton.

1. Living in the sunshine, bright and happy day, As I walk with Je-sus
2. Living in the sunshine, walking in the light, How my soul re-joic-es
3. Living in the sunshine, this is joy di-vine, Sweet the light of heaven
4. Living in the sunshine, sweet the life of praise, Growing up in Je-sus

all a-long the way, Holding sweet communion with my heav'nly King,
as I know my right; Cleans'd from all that's sinful, made as white as snow,
in my soul doth shine; And the path grows brighter as I on-ward go,
all the coming days; Watching for the Bridegroom, who will soon be here,

CHORUS.

O 'tis sweetest pleasure while his praise I sing.
O it is so glorious all God's will to know.
In my Lord I triumph o-ver ev-'ry foe.
In an hour we know not Je-sus will ap-pear.
} Living in the sunshine,

as I pass a-long, Glo-ri-fy-ing Je-sus, all my life a song; Finding

milk and honey, feeding on the best, O it is delightful in my Lord to rest.

Copyright, 1899, by Wm. J. Kirkpatrick.

PEACE IS MINE.

Morgan L. Williams. Welsh Melody. Arr. by M. L. W.

1. Grace di-vine, since thou didst find me, Peace, peace is mine;
2. Vain and fleet-ing is earth's pleasure, Peace, peace is mine;
3. While I serve my Lord and fear him, Peace, peace is mine;

Fears and doubts are left behind me, Peace, peace is mine.
Heav-en yon-der holds my treasure, Peace, peace is mine.
Ev-er striv-ing to be near him, Peace, peace is mine;

Satan's hosts have sore-ly tried me, But no harm can e'er betide me
When earth's cares shall vex and grieve me, Friends forsake, and loved ones leave me,
Naught of earth can ev-er waive me; By the grace my Saviour gave me,

While my Shepherd is be-side me; Peace, peace is mine.
Thou, O Saviour, wilt receive me, Peace, peace is mine.
By the blood he shed to save me, Peace, peace is mine.

Copyright, 1890, by Morgan L. Williams.

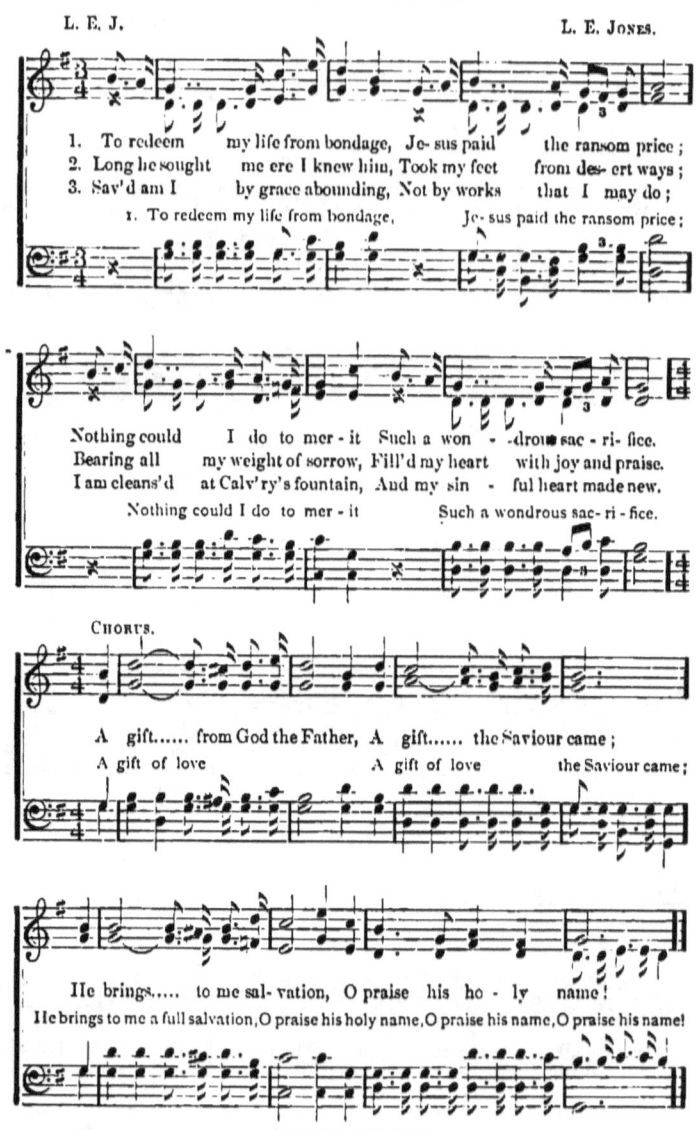

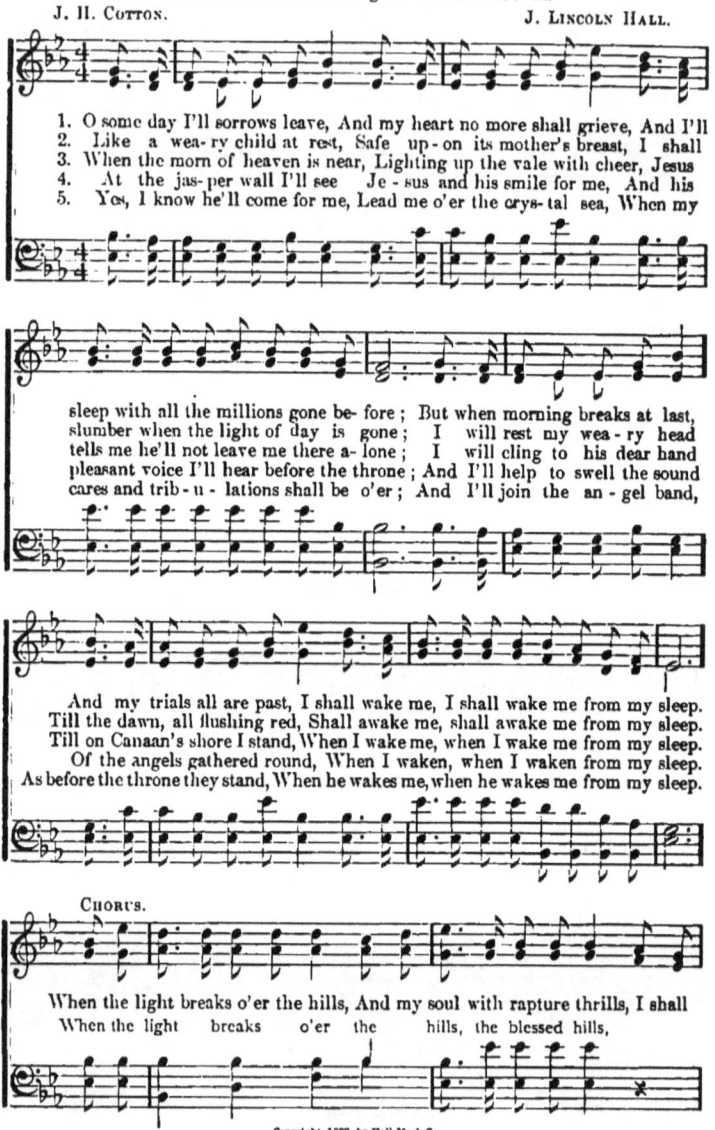

WHEN THE LIGHT BREAKS, Etc.—Concluded.

SAVE THEM TO-DAY.

H. A. K. Wm. J. Kirkpatrick.

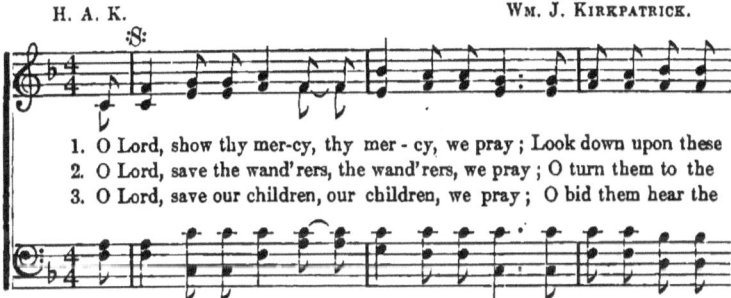

1. O Lord, show thy mer-cy, thy mer-cy, we pray; Look down upon these
2. O Lord, save the wand'rers, the wand'rers, we pray; O turn them to the
3. O Lord, save our children, our children, we pray; O bid them hear the

Chorus.—Save them to-day, Lord, save them to-day; Send down thy soul-con-

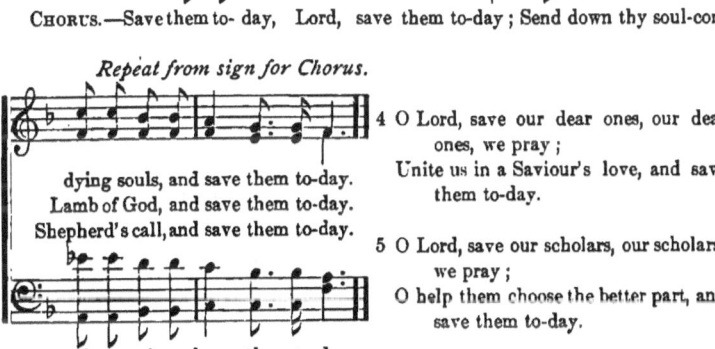

Repeat from sign for Chorus.

dying souls, and save them to-day.
Lamb of God, and save them to-day.
Shepherd's call, and save them to-day.

verting pow'r, and save them to-day.

4 O Lord, save our dear ones, our dear ones, we pray;
Unite us in a Saviour's love, and save them to-day.

5 O Lord, save our scholars, our scholars, we pray;
O help them choose the better part, and save them to-day.

Copyright, 1899, by Wm. J. Kirkpatrick.

HAVE YOU FOUND THE SAVIOUR PRECIOUS?

IDA L. REED.   J. LINCOLN HALL.

1. Have you found the Sav-iour pre-cious? More than all on earth be-side,
2. Have you found the Sav-iour pre-cious? Who for you passed thro' the grave,
3. Have you found the Sav-iour pre-cious? Do you know the peace and rest,
4. Have you found the Sav-iour pre-cious? Seek Him then with-out de-lay,

He who gave His life to save you, Who for your transgress-ions died?
Broke the bonds of death a-sun-der, Have you "proved His pow'r to save?"
That doth fill each soul that trusts Him; Who in His deep love is blest?
Taste the sweet-ness of His par-don, He will take our sins a-way.

CHORUS.

Have you found   the Sav-iour pre - cious? Can you
         Have you found,   found this friend? Can you

slight   such love as this, Sure-ly there can be no
slight, you slight, such love as this,   Sure-ly there can be no

great - er, Would you give   your life for His?
great - er love,   Would you, give your life for His? (for His?)

Copyright, 1897, by Hall-Mack Co.

38 ALL IN THY HANDS.

IDA L. REED.
J. LINCOLN HALL.

DUETT FOR SOPRANO AND TENOR OR ALTO.

1. All in Thy hands I leave, dear Lord, All of life's dai-ly fret and sting,
2. All in Thy hands each hour, each day, Whether cares may be great or small,
3. All in Thy hands my Lord and King, All of life's sor-row, toil and pain,
4. All in Thy hands O' rich re-ward, Peace and joy it doth bring to me,

All of my griefs whate'er they are, This to my soul sweet peace doth bring.
Je-sus, dear Lord, I lean on Thee, Thou art my ref-uge and my all.
All of my cares I bring to Thee, Thy love my soul will e'er sus-tain.
Dai-ly I rest in Thee, dear Lord, Dai-ly I'm lean-ing more on Thee.

CHORUS.

All in Thy hands like a glad re-frain, Com-eth the promise so sweet,

"Bring me Thy bur-den, I will sus-tain, Give to Thee strength complete."

Copyright, 1897, by Hall-Mack Co.

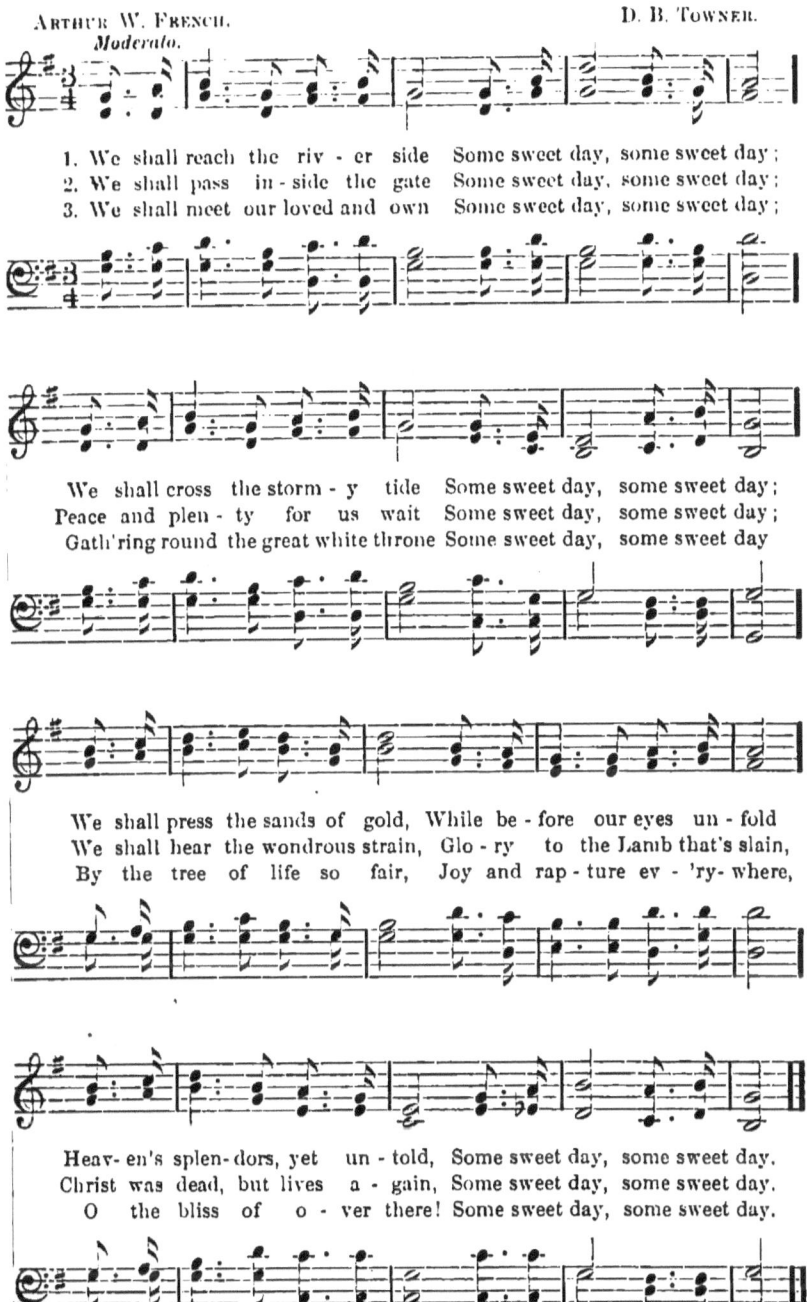

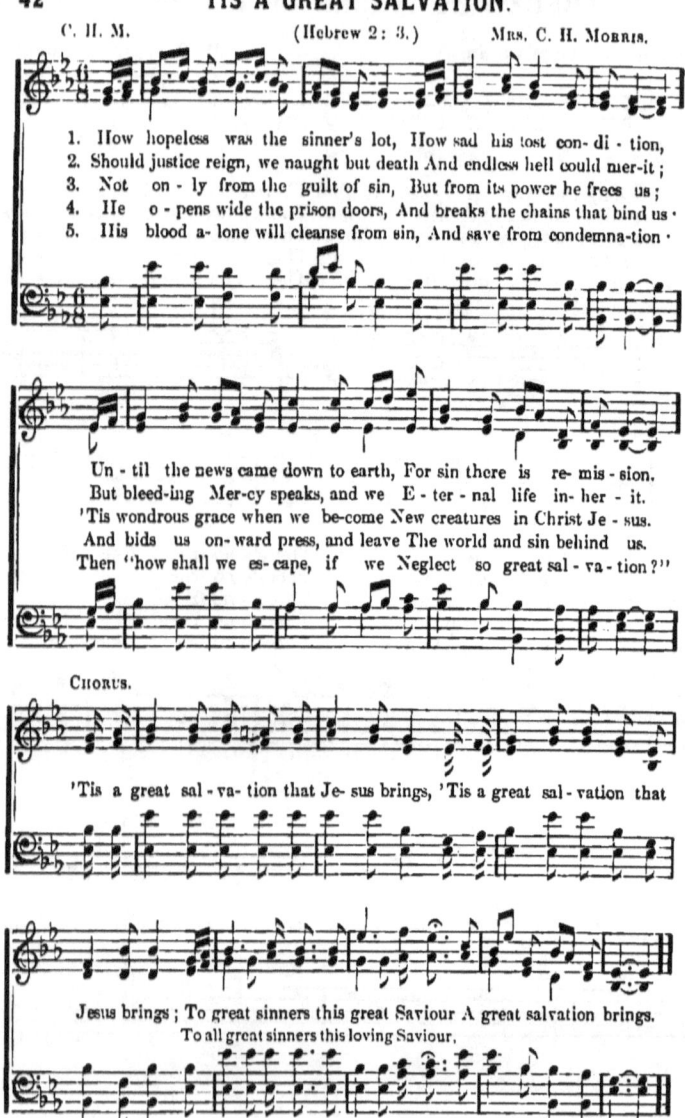

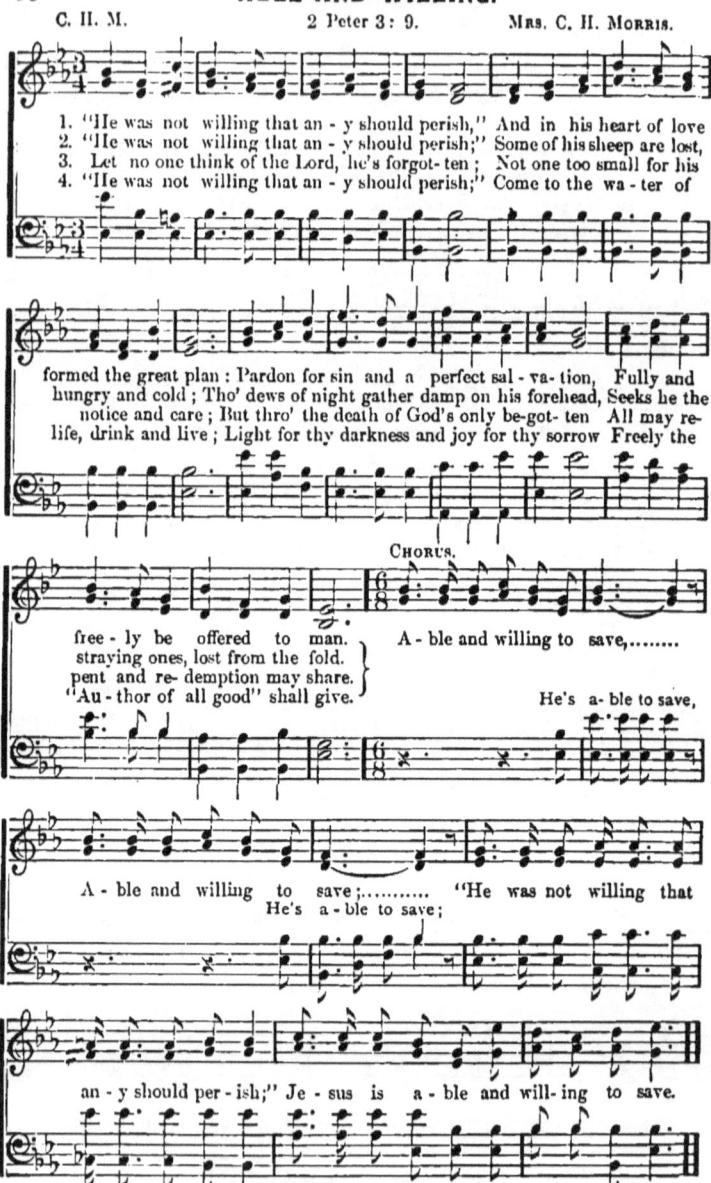

"PASSETH UNDERSTANDING." 51

E. E. H.
E. E. Hewitt.

1. O bless-ed tok-en of the Father's love, The peace that passeth under-
2. The world can neither give nor take a-way The peace that passeth under-
3. 'Tis founded on the liv-ing truth of God, The peace that passeth under-
4. Far better treasure than earth's fragile joys, The peace that passeth under-

stand-ing; My Sav-iour brought it from the land a-bove, The peace that
stand-ing; New measures Je-sus giv-eth day by day, The peace that
stand-ing; And by his Spir-it sweetly shed a-broad, The peace that
stand-ing; Sure pledge of heaven's ev-er-last-ing joys, The peace that

CHORUS.

passeth understand-ing. Blessed peace, O wondrous peace! May its swelling

tide increase, And with heav'nly music roll O'er my yielded soul.

Copyright, 1899, by Wm. J. Kirkpatrick.

NEVER ALONE.—Concluded.

Nev-er to leave me a-lone. Nev-er to leave me a-lone.

JESUS HAS LIFTED THE LOAD.

E. E. HEWITT. WM. J. KIRKPATRICK.

1. The trust-ing heart to Je-sus clings, Nor an - y ill for - bodes,
2. The pass-ing days bring ma - ny cares, "Fear not," I hear Him say,
3. He tells me of my Fa - ther's love, And nev - er-slumb'ring eye;
4. When to the throne of grace I flee, I find the prom-ise true,

But at the cross of Cal - v'ry, sings, Praise God for lift - ed loads!
And when my fears are turned to prayers, The bur-dens slip a - way.
My ev - er - last-ing King a - bove Will all my needs sup-ply.
The might-y arms up-hold - ing me Will bear my burdens too.

CHORUS.

Sing-ing I go a - long life's road, Praising the Lord, praising the Lord,

rit. ad lib.

Sing-ing I go a - long life's road, For Je-sus has lift-ed my load.

Copyright, 1896, by Wm. J. Kirkpatrick.

WHO IS THIS?—Concluded.

Bow before him, and adore him, Jesus Christ the mighty.... to save......
the mighty, the mighty to save.

ON LONE CALVARY.

C. E. F.   Chas. E. Ferguson.

1. On a lone, lone hill, call'd Calvary, The Saviour was cru-ci-fied;
2. There he suf-fer'd woe and pain untold, His head was bow'd down in shame;
3. Thou art still my Refuge, Saviour dear, Shelt'ring me from the storms that come;

It was there His blood was shed for me, From His pierced hands and side.
For a world so cru-el and so cold, Je-sus died—O praise His name!
All a-long life's journey be Thou near, 'Till I safe ar-rive at Home.

Chorus.

Was ev-er known such love as this—Such love how could there be!

I kneel in pray'r and thankfulness, To Him who died for me.

Copyright, 1899, by Wm. J. Kirkpatrick.

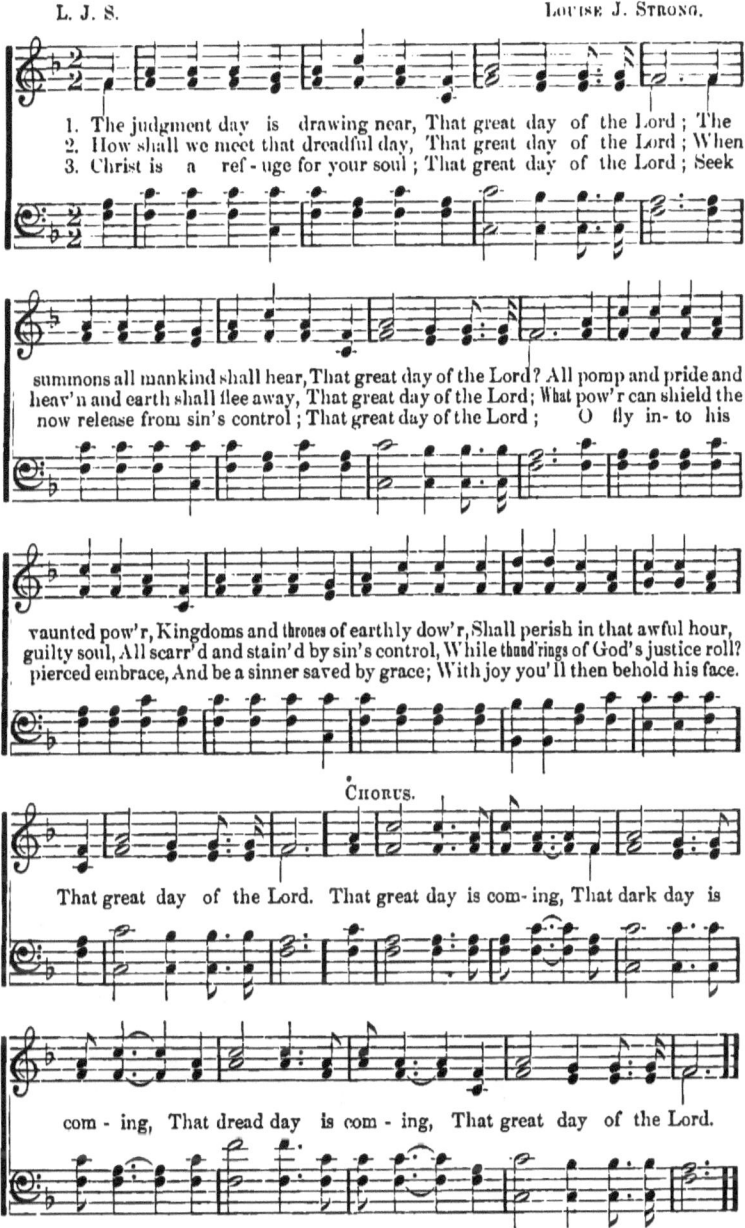

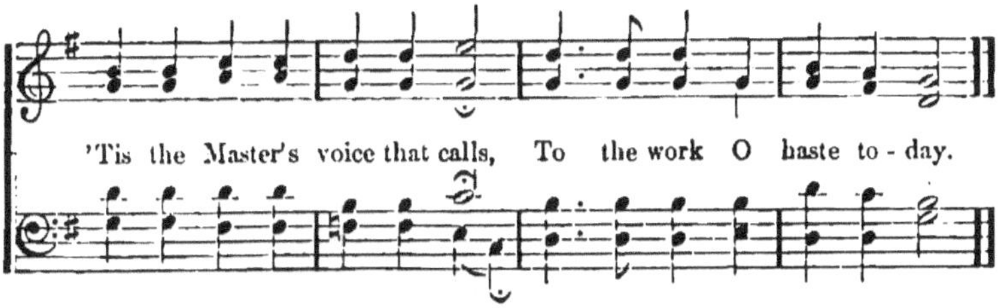

TO THE WORK.—Concluded.

'Tis the Master's voice that calls, To the work O haste to-day.

SWEET SUMMER LAND.

Rev. Johnson Oatman, Jr.   Howard. E. Smith.

1. In heav'n the skies are always bright, There's no *night* there; For our dear Saviour is the light, There's no night there. There's no night there, There's no night there, I long for thee, sweet summer land, There's no night there.
2. Tho' sor-row here may tear our breast, There's no *grief* there; There all is joy and peace and rest, There's no grief there. There's no grief there, There's no grief there, I long for thee, sweet summer land, There's no grief there.
3. What tho' we oft-en suf-fer here? There's no *pain* there; Our anguish soon will disappear, There's no pain there. There's no pain there, There's no pain there, I long for thee, sweet summer land, There's no pain there.
4. Tho' tears be-dew our pil-grim way, No *tears* are there; Our God will wipe them all away, No tears are there. No tears are there, No tears are there, I long for thee, sweet summer land, No tears are there.
5. No more from our dear friends we'll part, There's no *death* there; No last farewell will break the heart, There's no death there. There's no death there, There's no death there, I long for thee, sweet summer land, There's no death there.

Copyright, 1899, by Hall-Mack Co.

62. BEHOLD THE SAVIOUR STANDING.

FANNY J. CROSBY.   WM. J. KIRKPATRICK.

1. Be - hold the Saviour standing And knocking at the door; His
2. Be - hold the Saviour waiting To heal your brok-en heart, And
3. Be - hold the Saviour waiting To give your spir - it rest, Ac-

gentle voice is calling you to - day; And if you come repent- ant, And
bring you out of darkness in - to day; Then haste with joy and gladness To
cept his offered mercy while you may; His words of peace and comfort Will

give your wand'rings o'er, Your sins he will for - ev - er take a - way.
choose the bet - ter part, Your sins he will for - ev - er take a - way.
calm your troubled breast, Your sins he will for - ev - er take a - way.

CHORUS.

Your sins he will for- ev - er take a - way,............ Your sins he will for-
                for - ev-er take away,

ev - er take a - way;................ O hear his gen - tle pleading;
for - ev - er take a - way;

Copyright, 1899, by Wm. J. Kirkpatrick.

BEHOLD THE SAVIOUR STANDING.—Concluded.

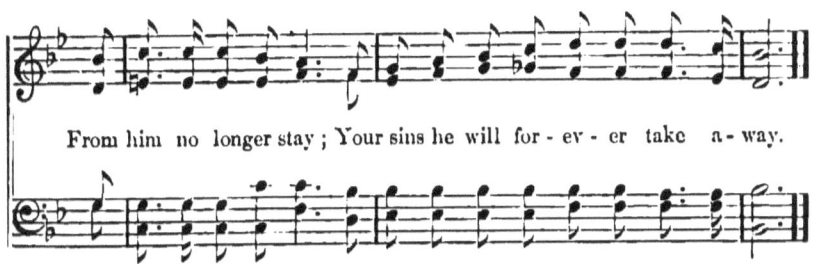

From him no longer stay; Your sins he will for-ev-er take a-way.

HOLD THOU MY HAND.

FANNY J. CROSBY.   WM. J. KIRKPATRICK.

1. Hold thou my hand, O Saviour, Hold thou my hand; Firm on the
2. Hold thou my hand, O Saviour, Keep thou my soul, When o'er a
3. Hold thou my hand, O Saviour, Till life is past; In-to the

rock e-ter-nal Help me to stand. There, in thy strength a-bid-ing;
troubled o-cean Storm billows roll. Lead thou the way be-fore me,
port of glo-ry Bring me at last. There, at the peaceful riv-er

There, in thy love confiding; Lord, in thy mercy hiding, Safe I shall be.
O let my faith adore thee; Then, with thy banner o'er me, Safe I shall be.
Where parting cometh never, With thy redeemed forever Safe I shall be.

Copyright, 1899, by Wm. J. Kirkpatrick.

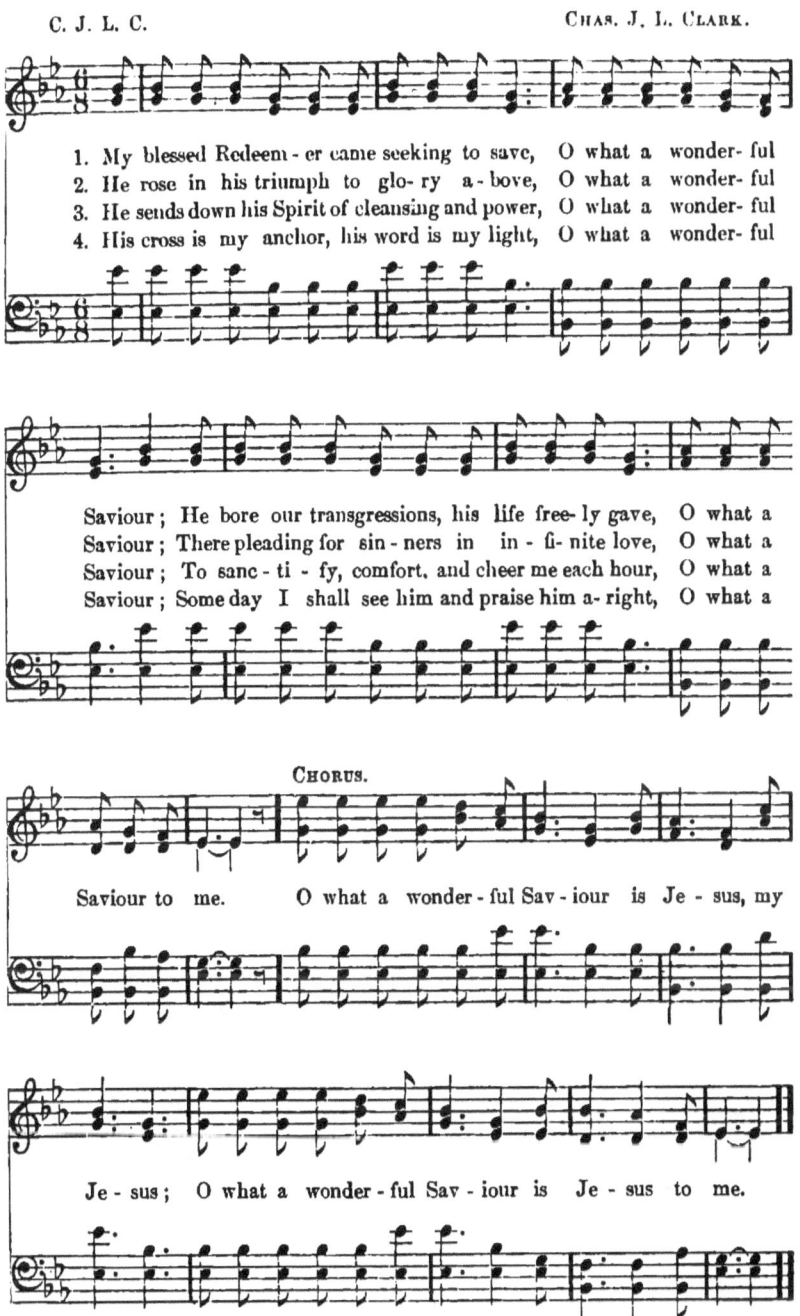

BE GALLANT IN THE FIGHT.
TO EPWORTH LEAGUES.

Chas. E. Ferguson. Wm. J. Kirkpatrick.

1. 'Neath His ban-ner bright we are march-ing to-day 'Neath the ban-ner of the cross we love; With His *word* our light shining on our way, Bright'ning all the path in which we rove.
2. In this no-ble cause may we prove ev-er true, Stand-ing firm-ly for the truth and right; Asking God to lead us in all we do, Triumph then shall crown us in the fight.
3. Let us fal-ter not tho' the foe may be near, With our shield and armor bright will stand; There are souls to save on the brink of death, In the res-cue let us lend a hand.

CHORUS.

Let us *look up* to Je-sus filled with His love, *Lift up* the fall-en to things a-bove; With Christ to lead us as we march along, Let us fight till we conquer ev'ry sin and wrong.

Copyright, 1899, by Wm. J. Kirkpatrick.

THE LORD IS MY LIGHT AND MY SALVATION. 71

R. O. Smith.   J. Lincoln Hall.

1. The Lord is my light and my sal-va-tion, Whom shall I fear?
2. The Lord is my light and my sal-va-tion, Glo-ry to God!
3. The Lord is my light and my sal-va-tion, Shout it a-gain;

Whom shall I fear?

He saves me from sin when in tempta-tion, For he's always near.
Now I would proclaim to ev-'ry na-tion, I'm saved by the blood.
And worthy our God of a-dor-a-tion, O join the re-frain.

He is always near, always near.
Saved by Jesus' blood, by the blood.
Join the glad refrain, glad refrain.

CHORUS.

The Lord is my light and my sal-va-tion, Glo-ry to God!

Glory to God!

The Lord is my light and my salva-tion, Of whom shall I be a-fraid?

Copyright, 1899, by Hall-Mack Co.

74. "THOU WILT KEEP HIM IN PERFECT PEACE."

Flora Kirkland.   Isa. 26 : 3.   Wm. J. Kirkpatrick.

1. The pal-ace of God's Per-fect Peace I can al-most dis-cern;
2. The sil-ver-shin-ing light of faith Grows bright and brighter still;
3. Hope fee-bly shone with-in my heart, While sad, I longed for rest;
4. O wondrous, wondrous peace of God! Thy ful-ness clos-es 'round;

The por-tal Trust I've safe-ly pass'd, No more for rest I yearn.
I know God's plans are best for me, I trust my Father's will.
But now Hope's light is clear and strong, This life of trust is best.
The por-tal Trust I've safe-ly pass'd, God's blessed peace I've found.

Chorus.

"Thou wilt keep him in perfect peace," Whose mind is stayed on Thee;

"Thou wilt keep him in perfect peace," Who trusts, yet can-not see.

Copyright, 1899, by Wm. J. Kirkpatrick.

82 CONQUERORS THROUGH THE BLOOD.

CONQUERORS THROUGH THE BLOOD. Concluded.

THE GRANDEST SONGS.

ALEXCENAH THOMAS. WM. J. KIRKPATRICK.

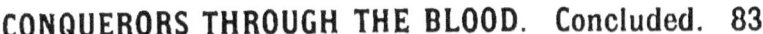

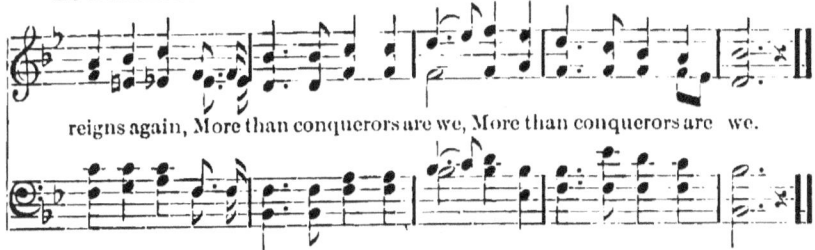

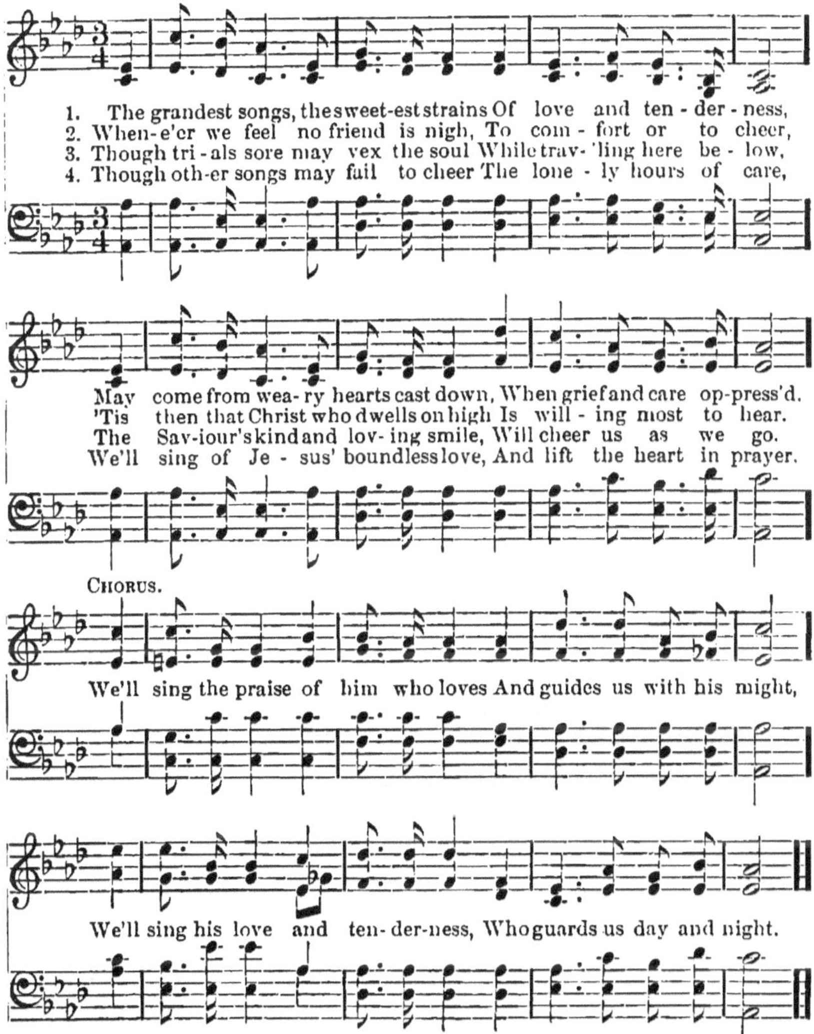

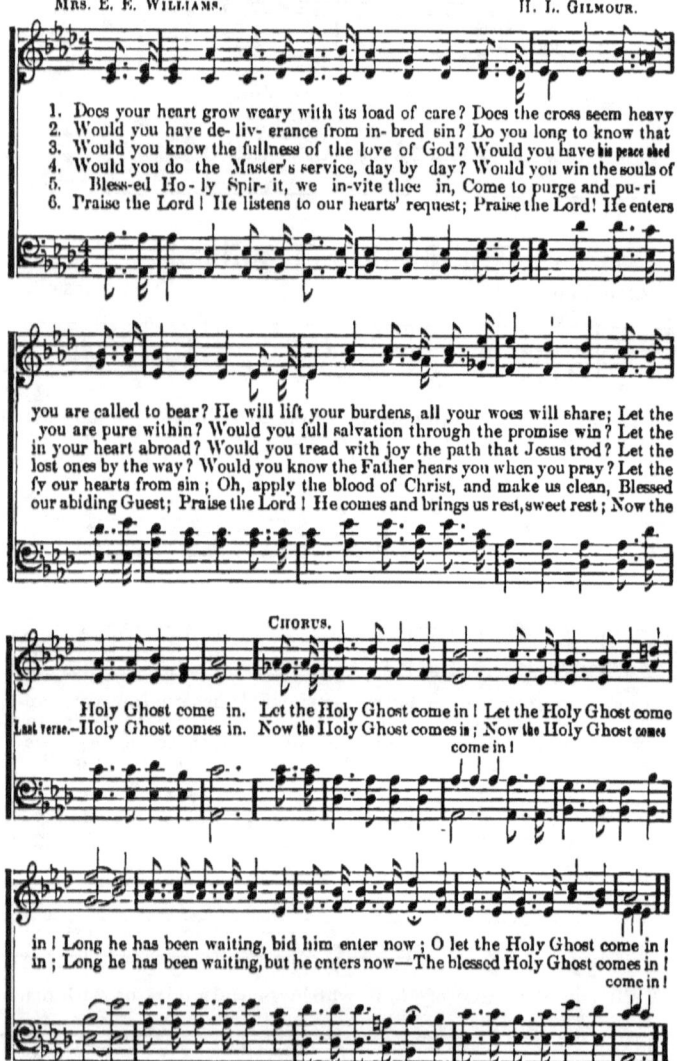

HIS LOVE CAN SATISFY.

L. E. J.   (Duet, or Quartet and Chorus.)   L. E. Jones.

1. O troubled heart,............ no long-er sigh,............ The love of
2. O fear-ful heart,............there's peace for thee,............ The blood ap-
3. O burdened heart,............ find rest from care,............ The Mas-ter

Christ........ can sat-is-fy;............ O come in faith,.......... and lowly
plied........ will set you free ;............ To Calv'ry's mount........ for cleansing
waits........ your load to bear ;............ Let ev-'ry grief............ to him be

bow,............ The Lord is here,............ receive him now..............
go,............And wash your robes.......... as white as snow..............
giv'n,............And trust his love............ for joy in heav'n..............

Chorus.

His love............ can satis-fy,   His love............ can satis-
His love can fully sat-is-fy, his love can satisfy, His love can fully sat-is-fy, his

fy ;........He speaketh peace, and sorrows cease, His love can satisfy............
love can satisfy ;   His love can fully satis-fy, can satisfy.

Copyright, 1899, by H. L. Gilmour.

JESUS' LOVE HAS MADE ME FREE. Concluded.

Ev - 'ry day my way grows brighter, Since his love has made me free.

BY AND BY.

IDA L. REED.   W. S. WEEDEN.

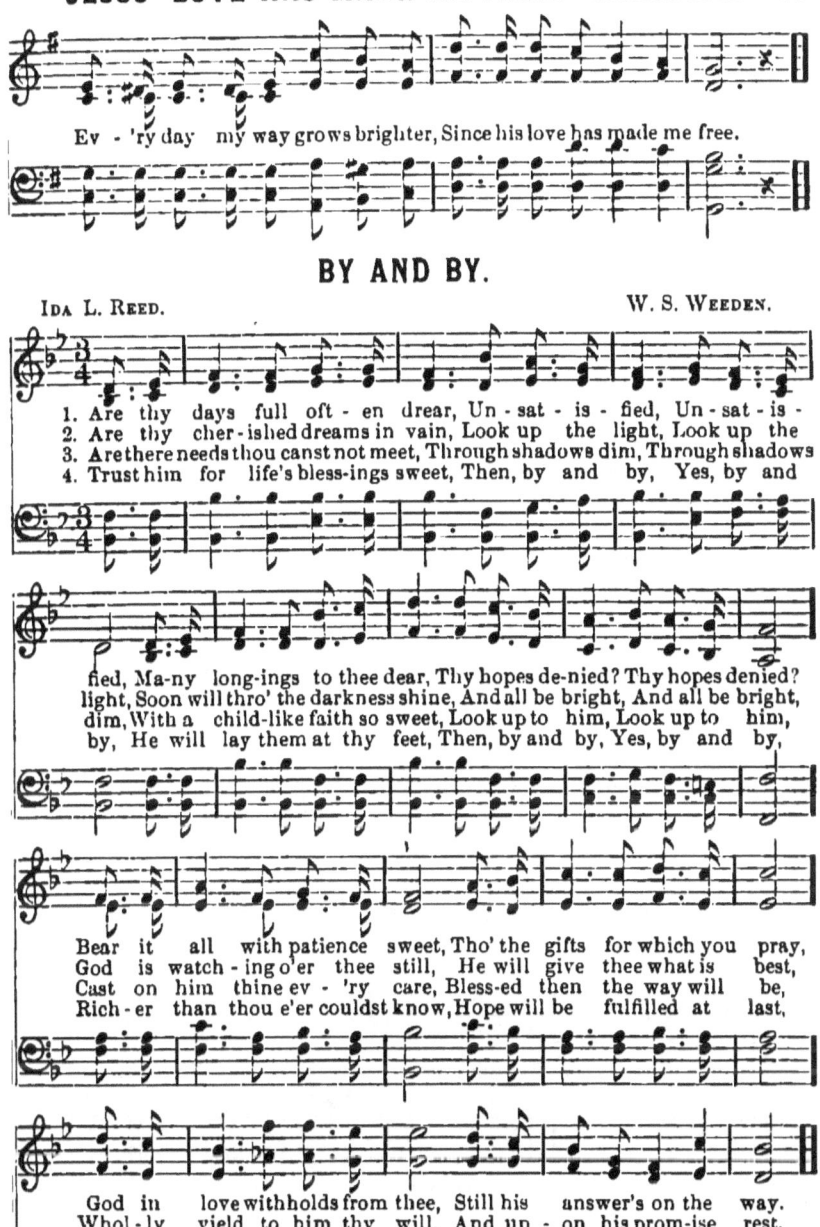

1. Are thy days full oft - en drear, Un - sat - is - fied, Un - sat - is -
2. Are thy cher - ished dreams in vain, Look up the light, Look up the
3. Are there needs thou canst not meet, Through shadows dim, Through shadows
4. Trust him for life's bless - ings sweet, Then, by and by, Yes, by and

fied, Ma-ny long-ings to thee dear, Thy hopes de-nied? Thy hopes denied?
light, Soon will thro' the darkness shine, And all be bright, And all be bright,
dim, With a child-like faith so sweet, Look up to him, Look up to him,
by, He will lay them at thy feet, Then, by and by, Yes, by and by,

Bear it all with patience sweet, Tho' the gifts for which you pray,
God is watch - ing o'er thee still, He will give thee what is best,
Cast on him thine ev - 'ry care, Bless-ed then the way will be,
Rich - er than thou e'er couldst know, Hope will be fulfilled at last,

God in love withholds from thee, Still his answer's on the way.
Whol - ly yield to him thy will, And up - on his prom-ise rest.
Glad - ly he thy griefs will bear, Ev - er - more he'll comfort thee.
Bless-ed joys will he be - stow, When the wait-ing time is past.

COMFORTER, IN MY HEART ABIDE.

L. E. J.   L. E. Jones.

1. Burdened with a load of sin, I seek for rest; Ho-ly Ghost di-
2. Ho-ly Ghost, make plain to me the writ-ten Word; Help me to ac-
3. May my life, O ho-ly one, thy presence know; May my face be

vine, come in, and be my guest; Come with fire, and quickly burn the dross away;
cept in faith, the blessed Lord; May my heart from evil passions be set free;
made to shine with love aglow; Take the cares I long have borne and give me peace;

CHORUS.

Make me pure and guide each day.
Give me joy and lib-er-ty. } Comforter, Comforter, in my heart a-bide;
Bid my sighing ev-er cease.

Give me peace, from sin release thro' Christ the cruci-fied; Comforter

Comforter, guide me all the way; Make me whole and fill my soul with praise each day.

Copyright, 1899, by H. L. Gilmour.

I AM SAVED BY FAITH IN JESUS.—Concluded.

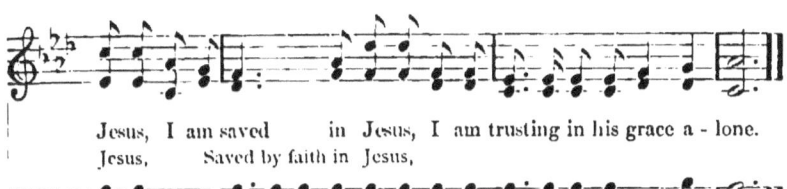

Jesus, I am saved in Jesus, I am trusting in his grace a-lone.
Jesus, Saved by faith in Jesus,

HE KNOWS IT ALL.

FANNY J. CROSBY.   (SOLO, DUET OR QUARTET.)   WM. J. KIRKPATRICK.

1. O heart bereaved and lonely, Whose brightest dreams have fled, Whose hopes like
2. O cling to thy Redeem- er, Thy Saviour, Brother, Friend; Believe and
3. Look up, the clouds are breaking, The storm will soon be o'er, And thou shalt

summer roses Are withered, crushed and dead, Tho' link by link is broken, And
trust his promise To keep thee to the end. O watch and wait with patience, But
reach the haven Where sorrows come no more. Look up, be not discouraged; Trust

tears unseen may fall, Look up amid thy sor-row To him who knows it all.
question not his will; His arms of love and mercy Are 'round about thee still.
on, whate'er befall; Remember, O re-member, Thy Saviour knows it all.

Copyright, 1890, by Wm. J. Kirkpatrick.

106. LEANING ON THE CROSS.

Rev. Johnson Oatman, Jr.   Howard E. Smith.

1. Since I heard my blessed Saviour call me, I am safe, whatev-er may be-
2. Tho' the storms of life may sweep around me, I am where they never will con-
3. Here the loving arms of Christ enfold me; Here his wisdom and his grace up-
4. Here thro' life I ever will keep standing, Till I hear the voice of death com-

fall me; So secure that nothing can ap-pall me; I'm leaning on the cross.
found me; I am where the hands of Christ hath bound me, I'm leaning on the cross.
hold me; Here I'm safe, the Comforter has told me; I'm leaning on the cross.
manding; But I'll shout when I have reached the landing, I'm leaning on the cross.

CHORUS.

Here the blessed Saviour died to save me; Here e-ter-nal life he free-ly

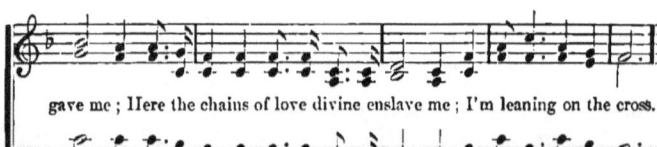

gave me; Here the chains of love divine enslave me; I'm leaning on the cross.

Copyright, 1899, by Hall-Mack Co.

108 GO FORWARD.

J. W. V.
J. W. Van Deventer.

1. A-rouse! ye men of war, Put on your ar-mor bright, And loy-al-ly, loy-al-ly De-fend the cause of right; The Cap-tain cries "to arms!" Let ev-'ry one o-bey, And earn-est-ly, earn-est-ly, Go forth to win the day.

2. The vic-to-ry is sure, The hosts of God will win, If loy-al-ly, loy-al-ly, We wage the war with sin Then press with vig-or on, Let noth-ing e'er dis-may But earn-est-ly, earn-est-ly, Go forth to win the day.

3. And when the cause is won, And war shall be no more, We'll joy-ful-ly, joy-ful-ly Pa-rade the oth-er shore; We'll sing the glad new song, Of grace so full and free, Shout vic-to-ry, vic-to-ry, Through-out e-ter-ni-ty.

CHORUS.

For-ward! for-ward! for-ward! to vic-to-ry, Firm-ly, bold-ly, pray-ing as you go, Be true and trust the Lord, De-

Copyright, 1899, by Hall-Mack Co.

GO FORWARD. Concluded.

pend up-on his word, Go for-ward, forward, And con-quer ev-'ry foe.

WHAT MAKES THE CHRISTIAN HAPPY?

IDA L. REED.   W. S. WEEDEN.

1. What makes the Christian hap-py, When clouds are ly - ing low, And
2. What makes him ev - er pa-tient, 'Neath per - se - cu-tion's flame, Brave
3. When ten - der ties are sev-ered, When heav - y sor-rows roll, A-

CHORUS.

thro' the shadowed val - ley, God call-eth him to go? } 'Tis that he knows the
'neath the wrongs he suffers, When bearing oth-er's blame. } (*Chorus for last verse.*)
cross his path what helps him, What then sustains his soul? } 'Tis this that makes him

Fa- ther, Is with him all the way, His hope and strength sustaining, His
hap - py, His God is ev - er near, His strength his soul sustaining, He

night is turned to day, His hope and strength sustaining, His night is turned to day.
takes a-way his fear, His strength his soul sustaining, He takes away his fear.

Copyright, 1899, by Hall-Mack Co.

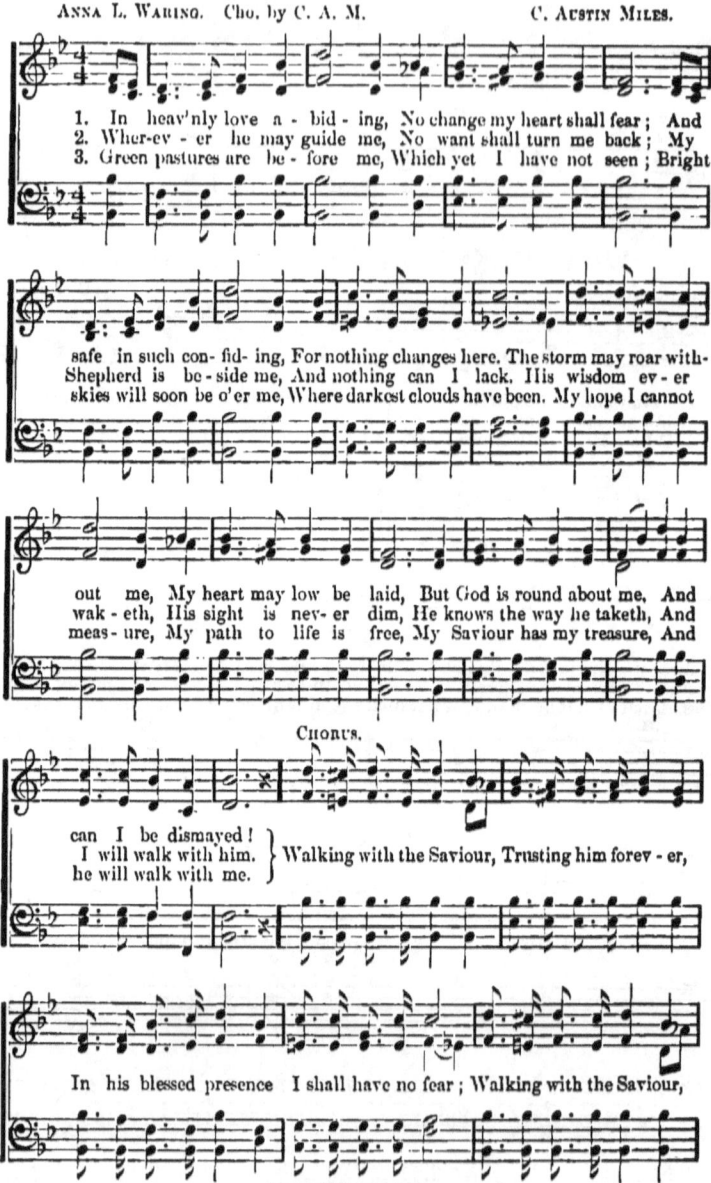

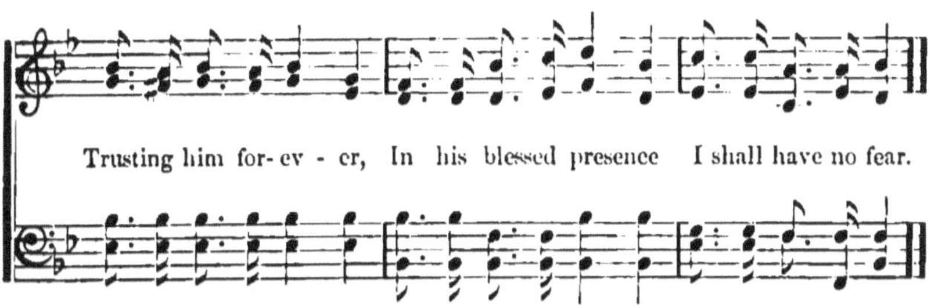

WALKING WITH THE SAVIOUR—Concluded.

Trusting him for-ev-er, In his blessed presence I shall have no fear.

VICT'RY ALL THE TIME.

L. E. J. L. E. Jones.

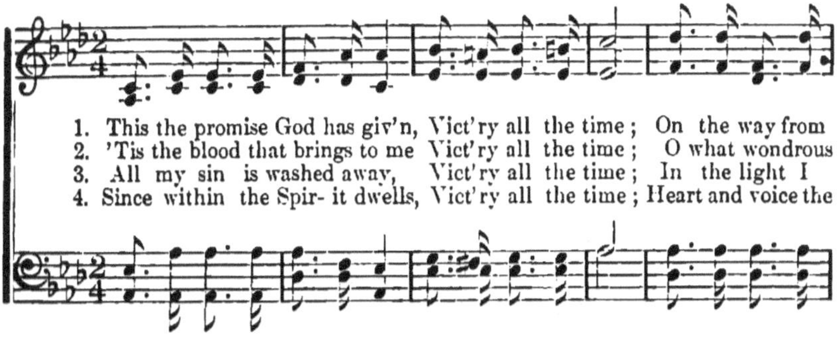

1. This the promise God has giv'n, Vict'ry all the time; On the way from
2. 'Tis the blood that brings to me Vict'ry all the time; O what wondrous
3. All my sin is washed away, Vict'ry all the time; In the light I
4. Since within the Spir-it dwells, Vict'ry all the time; Heart and voice the

CHORUS.

earth to heav'n, Vic-t'ry all the time.
lib-er-ty, Vic-t'ry all the time.
walk to-day, Vic-t'ry all the time.
cho-rus swells, Vic-t'ry all the time.

Vict'ry all the time, Vic-t'ry, vic-t'ry, all the time,

Vict'ry all the time; Jesus' blood, so wonderful, Gives vict'ry all the time.

Copyright, 1899, by H. L. Gilmour.

JESUS SAVES ME, JESUS SAVES.

Mrs. Frank A. Breck. Wm. J. Kirkpatrick.

1. I have found a great sal-va-tion, Je-sus saves me, Je-sus saves;
2. Gone is all my care and sad-ness, Je-sus saves me, Je-sus saves;
3. Je-sus' love is true and ten-der, Je-sus saves me, Je-sus saves;

He is all my con-so-la-tion, Je-sus saves me, Je-sus saves.
He has filled my soul with gladness, Je-sus saves me, Je-sus saves.
For his love what can I ren-der? Je-sus saves me, Je-sus saves.

He has washed my sins a-way; He will ev-er with me stay;
I was bound, he set me free; I was blind, he made me see;
I will give my life, my all; I will go where he may call;

Blessed peace is mine to-day; Je-sus saves me, Je-sus saves.
O how great his grace to me! Je-sus saves me, Je-sus saves.
I will trust, whate'er be-fall; Je-sus saves me, Je-sus saves.

Copyright, 1899, by Wm. J. Kirkpatrick.

YOU MAY HAVE THE JOYBELLS.—Concluded. 115

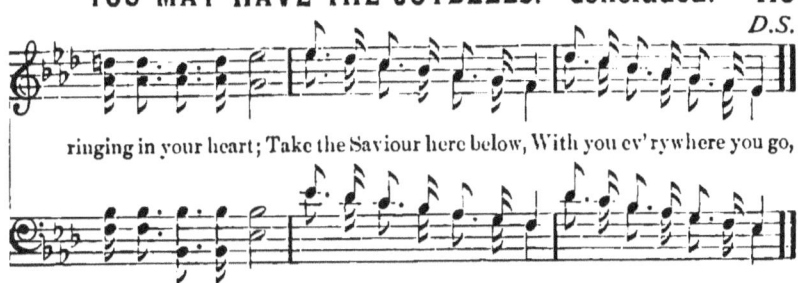

ringing in your heart; Take the Saviour here below, With you ev'rywhere you go,

MAKE ME A CHILD OF THINE.

E. E. Hewitt. (Solo or Duet.) Wm. J. Kirkpatrick.

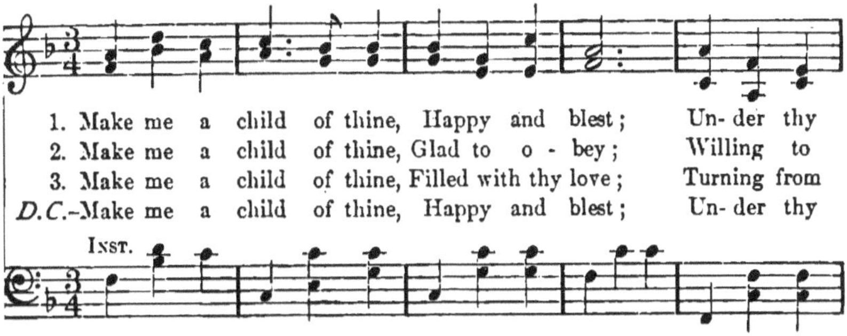

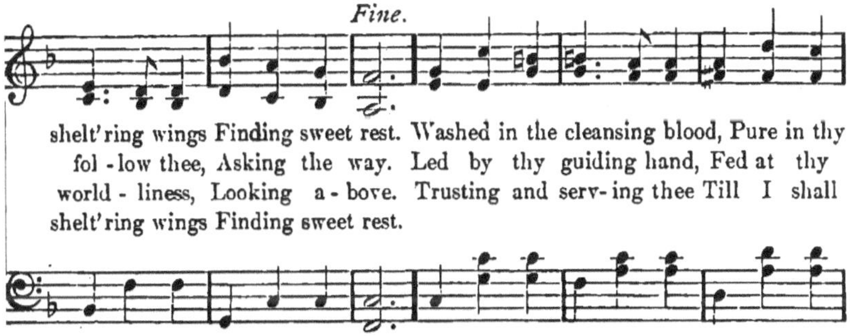

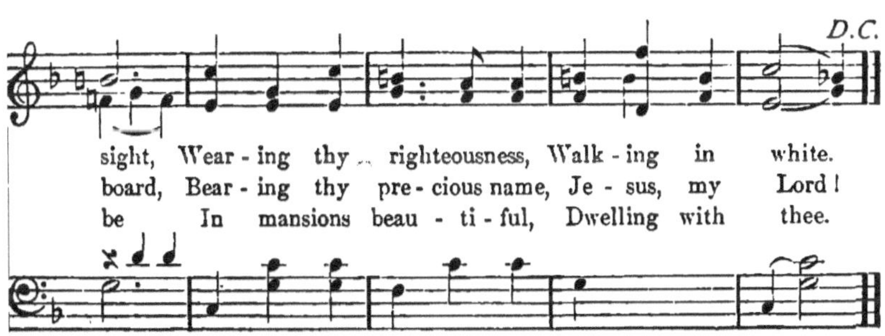

1. Make me a child of thine, Happy and blest; Un-der thy
2. Make me a child of thine, Glad to o-bey; Willing to
3. Make me a child of thine, Filled with thy love; Turning from
D.C.—Make me a child of thine, Happy and blest; Un-der thy

shelt'ring wings Finding sweet rest. Washed in the cleansing blood, Pure in thy
fol-low thee, Asking the way. Led by thy guiding hand, Fed at thy
world-liness, Looking a-bove. Trusting and serv-ing thee Till I shall
shelt'ring wings Finding sweet rest.

sight, Wear-ing thy righteousness, Walk-ing in white.
board, Bear-ing thy pre-cious name, Je-sus, my Lord!
be In mansions beau-ti-ful, Dwelling with thee.

Copyright, 1899, by Wm. J. Kirkpatrick.

4 But we never can prove
The delights of his love
Until all on the altar we lay,
For the favor he shows,
And the joy he bestows,
Are for all who will trust and obey.

5 Then in fellowship sweet
We will sit at his feet,
Or we'll walk by his side in the way;
What he says we will do,
Where he sends we will go,
Never fear, only trust and obey.

120 SWEET LAND OF BLISS.

JESSE P. TOMPKINS. CHAS. BENTLEY.

1. Sometimes, in hours when all is still, The land of love around me lies,
2. Sometimes the way seems all a-glow With light ce-les-tial from the sky,
3. Sometimes I seem to see the face Of him who is my soul's delight;
4. Sometimes I seem to catch the song That falls from lips that live in light,

And leaves its im-press on my will, Tho' hidden from these mortal eyes.
And in my soul I feel and know That an-gel forms are ev-er nigh.
And as I gaze in-to those eyes, My soul is filled with radiance bright.
And then, in silence, how I long For that blest gift—immortal sight.

CHORUS.

Sweet land of bliss, not far a-way, I love to think, as here I stay,

That silence sometimes brings me near To that blest land to me so dear.

Copyright, 1899, by Wm. J. Kirkpatrick.

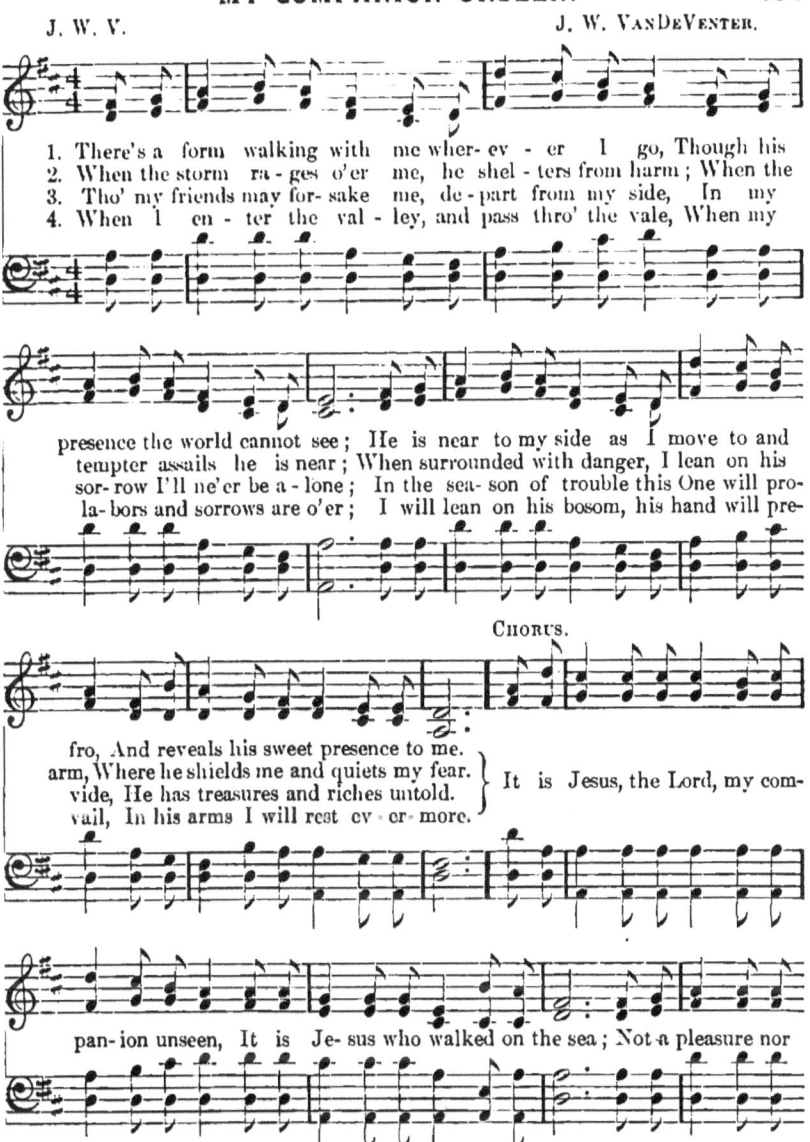

PERFECT TRUST IN THEE.

FANNIE J. CROSBY. ALVIN S. CLARK.

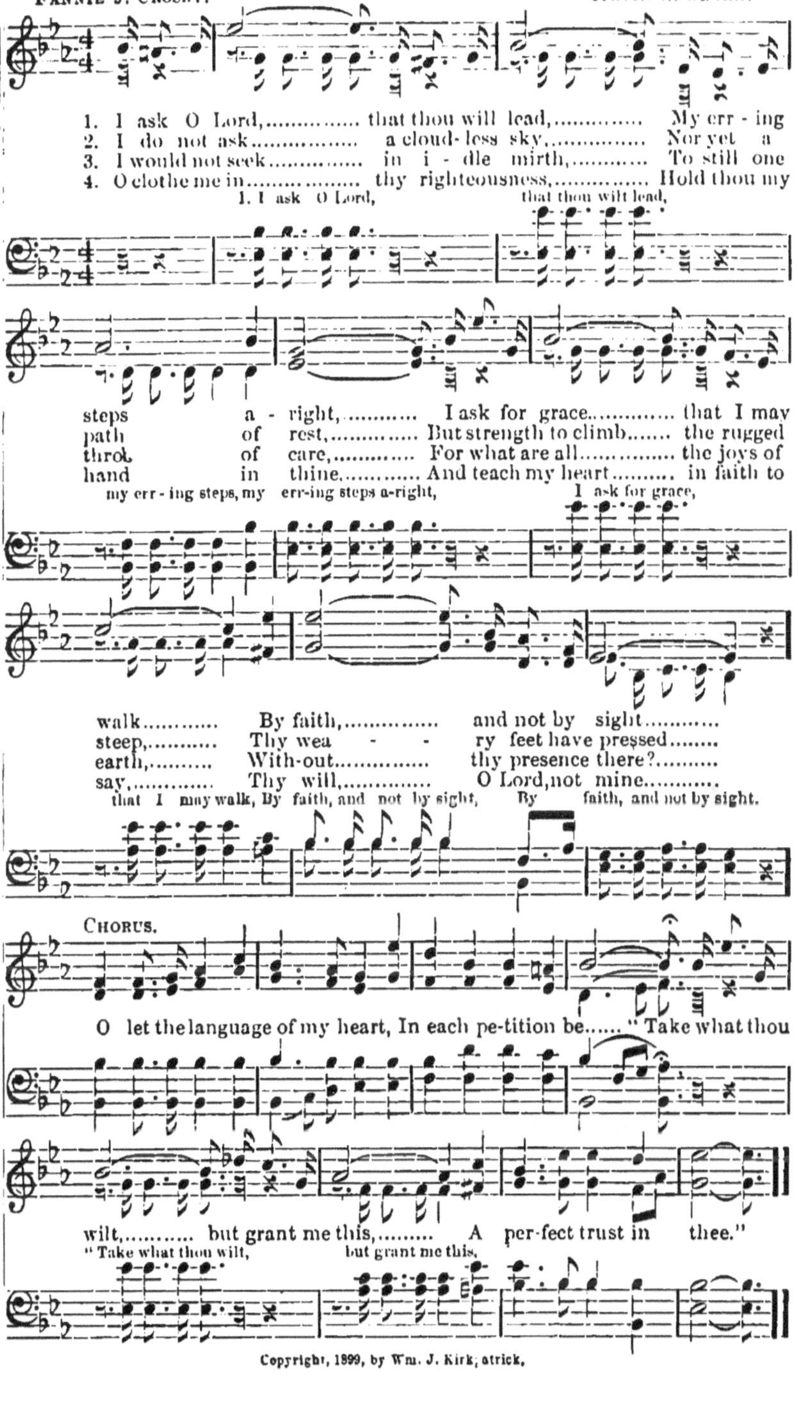

WAITING FOR THE KING. Concluded.

hap - py day will the shadows pass away, At the com - ing of the King.

RINGING SWEETLY ON THE QUIET AIR.

C. A. M.
C. Austin Miles.

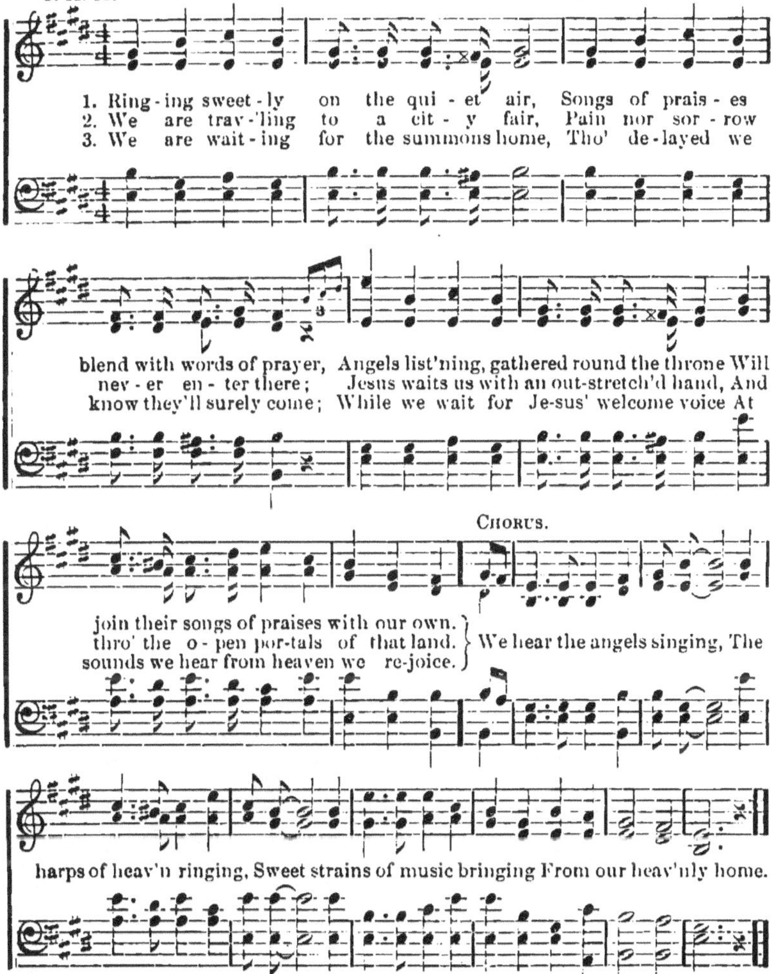

1. Ring - ing sweet - ly on the qui - et air, Songs of prais - es
2. We are trav - 'ling to a cit - y fair, Pain nor sor - row
3. We are wait - ing for the summons home, Tho' de - layed we

blend with words of prayer, Angels list'ning, gathered round the throne Will
nev - er en - ter there; Jesus waits us with an out-stretch'd hand, And
know they'll surely come; While we wait for Je-sus' welcome voice At

CHORUS.

join their songs of praises with our own.
thro' the o - pen por-tals of that land. } We hear the angels singing, The
sounds we hear from heaven we re-joice.

harps of heav'n ringing, Sweet strains of music bringing From our heav'nly home.

Copyright, 1899, by Hall-Mack Co.

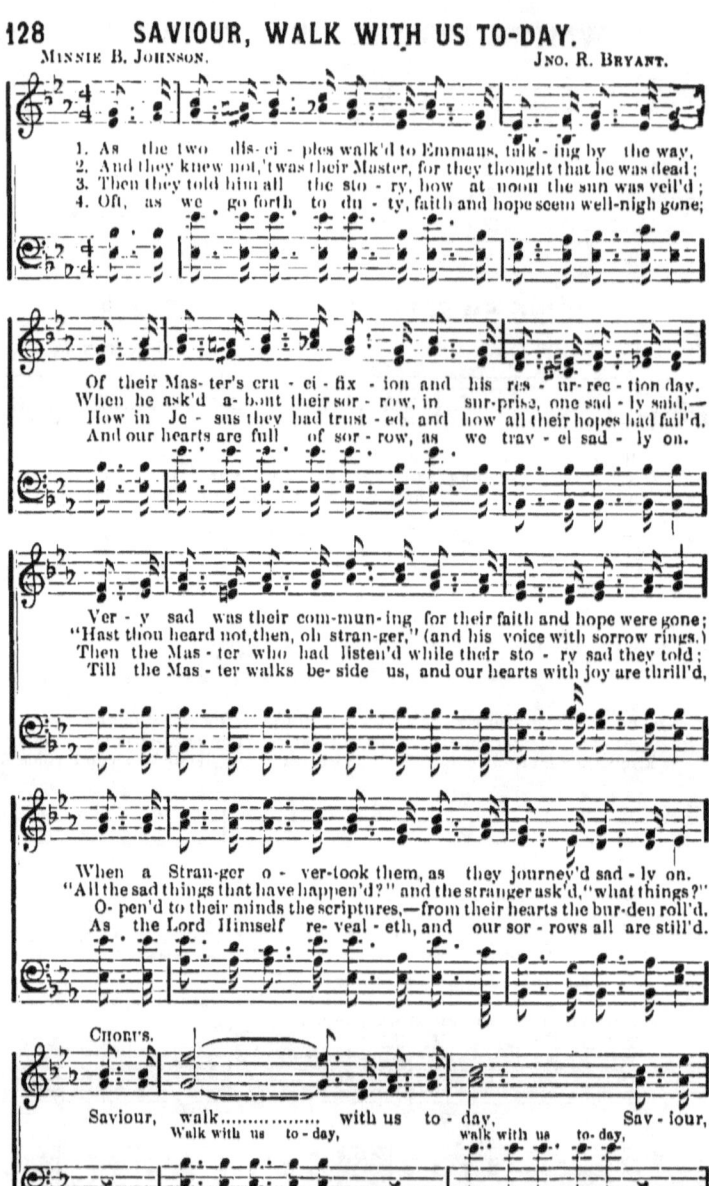

TO HIM BE GLORY. Concluded.

Christ the lamb was slain, To him be glo-ry, hon-or, pow'r, Forever, A - men.

"I HAVE PRAYED FOR THEE."

"Satan hath desired to have you, that he may sift you as wheat: but I have prayed for thee, that thy faith fail not:"—Jesus.

Mrs. MARY B. WINGATE.   H. L. GILMOUR.

1. "I have prayed for thee, that thy faith fail not," O words of the Christ di - vine:
2. "I have prayed for thee, that thy faith fail not," O words that will cheer and bless,
3. "I have prayed for thee, that thy faith fail not," The Fath - er will answer prayer;
4. "I have prayed for thee, that thy faith fail not," When crossing the mys-tic tide;

In times of troub-le, doubt or fear, I claim the sweet message mine.
When foes combine or storms may come, Or burdens of life op - press.
And ten-der-ly keep the trusting one, The child of his love and care.
I'll whis-per it soft-ly o'er and o'er, And cling to my bless-ed Guide.

CHORUS.

"Sa-tan hath desired to have you, That he may sift you as wheat: But I have prayed for thee, I have prayed for thee, That thy faith fail not."

Copyright, 1899, by H. L. Gilmour, Wenonah, N. J.

132. FILL UP THE RANKS FOR JESUS.

C. H. M.
Mrs. C. H. Morris.

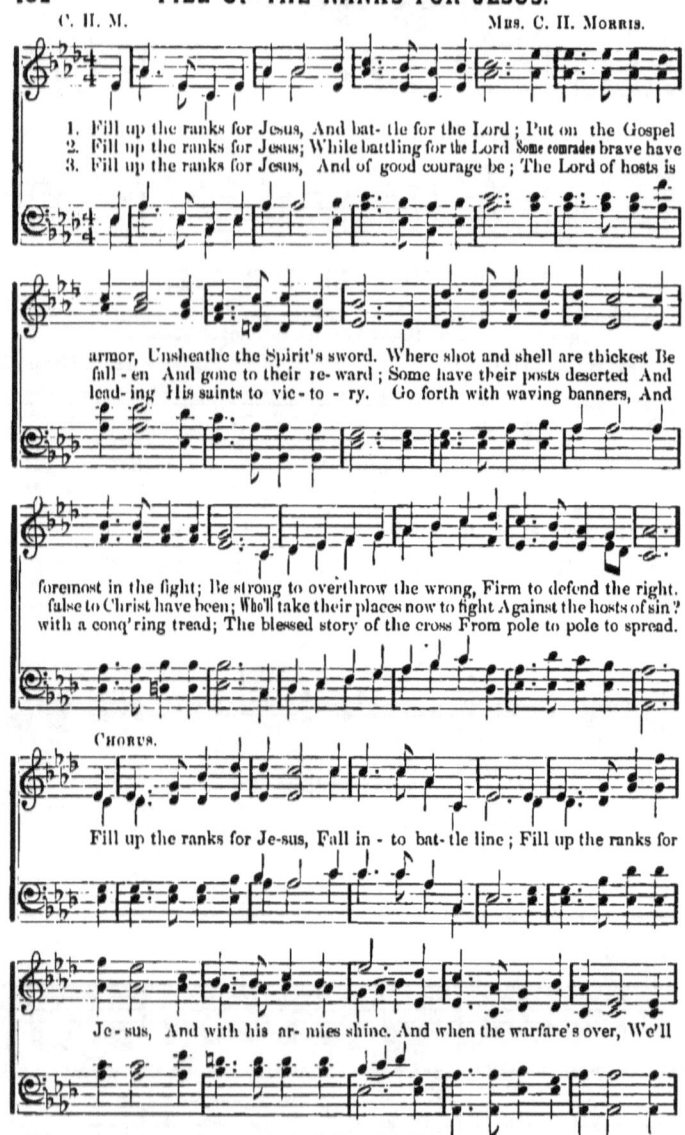

1. Fill up the ranks for Jesus, And bat-tle for the Lord; Put on the Gospel armor, Unsheathe the Spirit's sword. Where shot and shell are thickest Be foremost in the fight; Be strong to overthrow the wrong, Firm to defend the right.
2. Fill up the ranks for Jesus; While battling for the Lord Some comrades brave have fall-en And gone to their re-ward; Some have their posts deserted And false to Christ have been; Who'll take their places now to fight Against the hosts of sin?
3. Fill up the ranks for Jesus, And of good courage be; The Lord of hosts is lead-ing His saints to vic-to-ry. Go forth with waving banners, And with a conq'ring tread; The blessed story of the cross From pole to pole to spread.

CHORUS.

Fill up the ranks for Je-sus, Fall in-to bat-tle line; Fill up the ranks for Je-sus, And with his ar-mies shine. And when the warfare's over, We'll

Copyright, 1899, by H. L. Gilmour.

FILL UP THE RANKS FOR JESUS.—Concluded.

lay our armor down; With Christ the Lord forever We'll wear the victor's crown.

STAY MY MIND ON THEE.

Mrs. Mary B. Wingate. Wm. J. Kirkpatrick.

Gracefully.

1. When the morning light shall dawn, Stay my mind on thee; When the evening
2. When the world would draw aside, Stay my mind on thee; When I feel its
3. When I stand be-side the tomb, Stay my mind on thee; When I feel its

hour comes on, Stay my mind on thee. When the cares of life increase,
pomp and pride, Stay my mind on thee. When the tempter hov-ers near,
chill and gloom, Stay my mind on thee. When I draw life's lat-est breath,

When my earthly comforts cease, Stay my mind on thee, Stay my mind on thee.
When I feel a doubt or fear, Stay my mind on thee, Stay my mind on thee.
When I yield myself in death, Stay my mind on thee, Stay my mind on thee.

Copyright, 1900, by Wm. J Kirkpatrick.

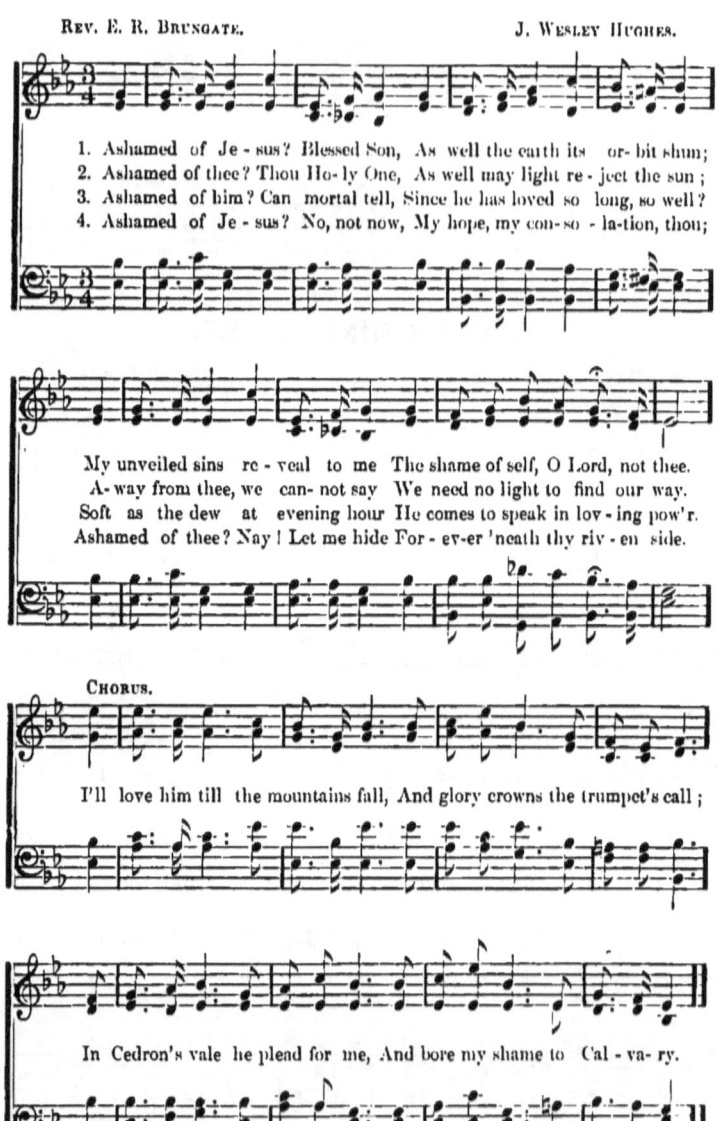

HE'LL NEVER FORSAKE.

Frank H. Mashaw. J. Lincoln Hall.

1. "I will fail thee never;" blessed words of cheer, Like a blaze of glo-ry,
2. "I will fail thee never;" tho' the night be long; Soon the morning cometh
3. "I will fail thee never;" brightest flow'rs will fade, But my trust in Jesus
4. "I will fail thee never;" fails the earth and sky, But his bow of promise

shining far and near; Tho' the storm and tempest all around may shake,
with its light and song; Precious words of comfort to my heart I take;
ne'er shall be betrayed; Midnight all around me, soon his light will break,
shineth still on high; Earthly sunbeams vanish, and my heart may quake,

Je-sus, my Saviour, has promised that he will nev-er for-sake.

CHORUS.

No, he'll never for-sake,...... No, he'll never for-sake;.... Dangers a-
Never forsake, Never forsake;

round me may threaten, Jesus will never forsake. :‖ Jesus will never forsake.

Copyright, 1909, by Hall-Mack Co.

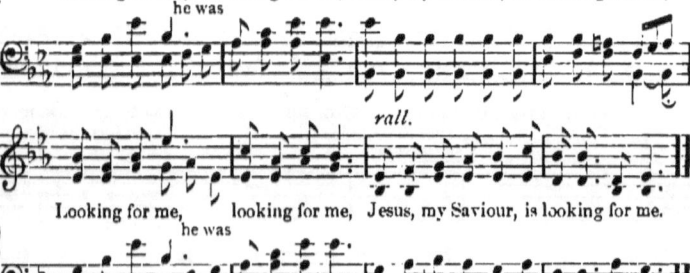

SPEAK A WORD.

139

J. W. V.
J. W. VanDeVenter.

1. Who will tes - ti - fy for Je - sus? Boldly stand and say a word?
2. Have you heard the Saviour knocking? Did you yield and let him in?
3. Are you now up- on the al - tar? Are you will - ing to o - bey?
4. Have you la - bored in the vineyard? Kindly give a word of cheer,

Who will heed the in - vi - ta - tion? Dare to rise and own their Lord?
Tell us when the door was opened, When he took a - way your sin.
Are you read - y for the har - vest, At your feet or far a - way?
It will be a source of bless - ing To the weak and wea - ry here.

CHORUS.

Speak a word, a word for Je - sus, Let your hope in God be known;

Bear the cross and tell the sto - ry, Dare to rise and stand a - lone.

Copyright, 1899, by Hall-Mack Co.

HIDDEN RICHES. Concluded.

But the bless-ed Ho-ly Spir-it, Hath these wondrous truths revealed.

EVERY STEP MY SAVIOUR COUNTS.

"Doth not He see my ways, and count all my steps?"—Job 21: 4.

E. E. HEWITT. WM. J. KIRKPATRICK.

1. Ev-'ry step my Sav-iour counts, All my ways are known to him,
2. Count-ing ev-'ry step I take, Ev-er watchful, ev-er near.
3. Ev-'ry wea-ry length he knows, Ev-'ry dark and rug-ged steep;
4. Not one step with-out my Guide, Not one hour with-out his love;

Paths that spark-le in the light, Those with shadows, gray and dim.
As the sun-beam melts the flake, May his look dis-pel all fear.
But he whis-pers hope and cheer, He will save me, he will keep.
He will bring me, in good time, To the bless-ed Home a-bove.

CHORUS.

I will trust him all the jour-ney, Step by step, and mile by mile;

Safe, his might-y arms are round me, Peaceful for I see his smile.

Copyright, 1899, by Wm. J. Kirkpatrick.

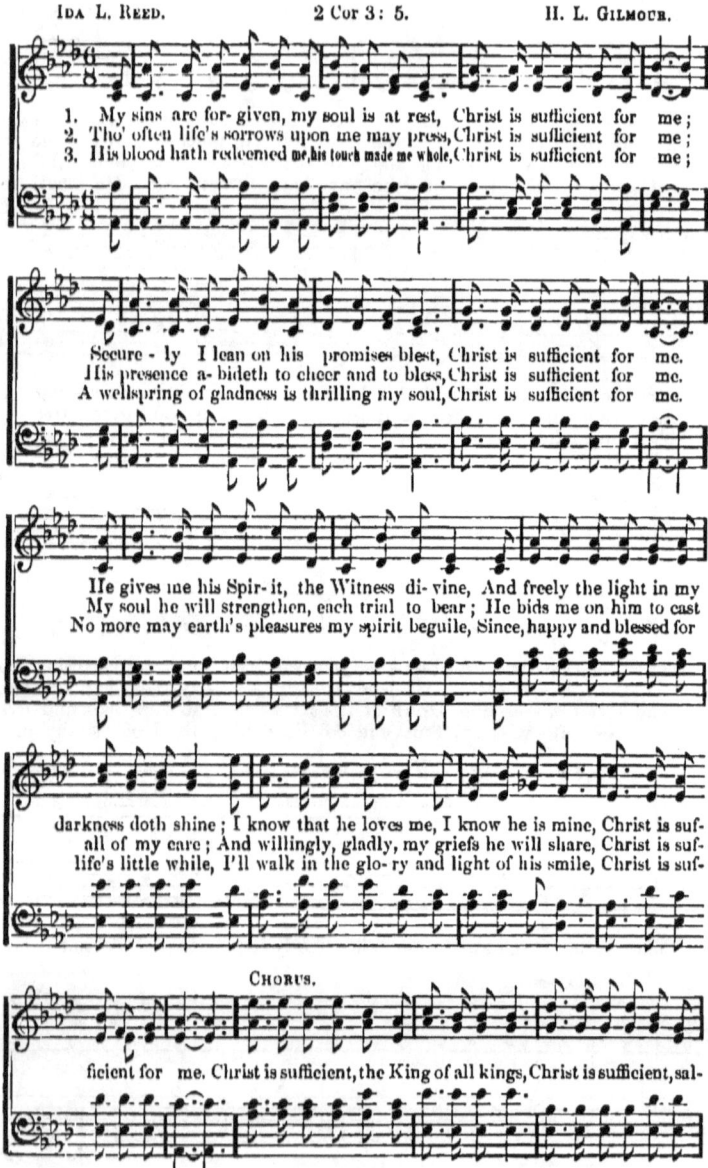

CHRIST IS SUFFICIENT.—Concluded.

vation he brings; Christ is sufficient, my happy soul sings, Christ is sufficient for me.

A WAVE OF SALVATION.

ANNIE S. HAWKS.   WM. J. KIRKPATRICK.

1. O Lord, send a wave of sal-va-tion Over our souls, over our souls;
2. O send like a wave of the o-cean, Even this hour, even this hour;
3. O quicken us, Lord, by thy Spir-it, Heal us within, heal us within;

We'll praise thee and give ador-a-tion While ev-er onward it rolls.
Sub-duing all strife and commo-tion, Gracious and mighty in pow'r.
By grace we are saved thro' thy merit, Cleanse us and keep us from sin.

CHORUS.

Send, Lord, a wave of sal-vation; Hear us, we pray, make no de-lay;

Send, Lord, a wave of sal-va-tion O-ver our souls to-day.

Copyright, 1899, by Wm. J. Kirkpatrick.

146 WHY NOT BE A HELPER?

J. W. H.
J. WESLEY HUGHES.

1. There's man-y a soul will per - ish, For want of friendly aid,
2. The Master hath need of help - ers, He calls for you to - day;
3. Then res- cue a soul for Je - sus, If on - ly one soul it be;
4. If on - ly a cup of wa - ter Be giv - en in Je - sus' name
5. Re- member, the greatest val - or Not on - ly claims re - nown,

Whom Je - sus has died to ran - som; Their full re - demption paid!
Then answer the summons glad - ly, Thy ser - vice he'll re - pay.
'Twill bring thee a hallowed pleas - ure To all e - ter - ni - ty!
To one who is faint and wea - ry, It shall not be in vain.
But low - li- est deeds of kind - ness Will gem thy glo - ry crown!

CHORUS.

Then why not be a help - er, Some precious soul to win?

Then why not be a help - er, To bring the lost ones in?

Copyright, 1899, by Hall-Mack Co.

EVERY WORD I BELIEVE.

Rev. Johnson Oatman, Jr.
Wm. J. Kirkpatrick.

Moderato.

1. If you ask me why I'm hap-py as I jour-ney down life's road,
2. We are not al-lowed to wan-der thro' this world with-out a Guide,
3. He in-forms us for our com-fort that thro' life he'll be our Friend,
4. He has told us of a cit-y where the streets are paved with gold,

Why it is I do not car-ry on the way a heav-y load,
For, to keep our feet from stray-ing his own word has been ap-plied,
That if we will on-ly trust him he'll go with us to the end,
Where the faithful shall be gath-ered and their Saviour's face be-hold,

It's because my Sav-iour tells me that my bur-den he'll re-ceive,
And we read there that the sentence of a sin-ner he'll re-prieve,
That his Spir-it will be with us while we do not slight nor grieve,
He has promised at its por-tals that our souls he will re-ceive,

CHORUS.

And I believe it, ev-'ry word I believe. I believe it, ev'ry
  And I   I be-lieve......

word I believe, I receive it, ev'ry word I receive; Je-sus tells me my
              I re-ceive...

wants he will relieve, And I believe it, ev-'ry word I believe.
              And I

Copyright, 1899, by Wm. J. Kirkpatrick.

150 GOD WILL TAKE CARE OF ME.

E. E. Hewitt.   Wm. J. Kirkpatrick.

1. God will take care of me; Here will I rest, Trusting his promise true, Safe on his breast. Changeful may be my lot, His mercy changeth not; No child of his forgot, In Jesus, blest.
2. God will take care of me, Hushing my fear; When dangers 'round I see, His voice I hear; Then let my soul be brave, High tho' the wind and wave, Greater his pow'r to save, Tenderly near.
3. God will take care of me, Holding the helm; Storms that may sweep the sea Will not o'erwhelm. Soon, ev-'ry billow passed, I shall my anchor cast, Safe, safe at home at last, In joy's bright realm.

Copyright, 1899, by Wm. J. Kirkpatrick.

NEARER, MY GOD, TO THEE.

Tune above.

1 Nearer, my God, to thee!
   Nearer to thee,
E'en though it be a cross
   That raiseth me;
Still all my song shall be,
‖: Nearer, my God, to thee, :‖
   Nearer to thee !

2 Though like the wanderer,
   The sun gone down,
Darkness be over me,
   My rest a stone,
Yet in my dreams I'd be
‖: Nearer, my God, to thee, :‖
   Nearer to thee !

3 There let the way appear
   Steps unto heaven ;
All that thou sendest me,
   In mercy given ;

Angels to beckon me
‖: Nearer, my God, to thee, :‖
   Nearer to thee !

4 Then, with my waking thoughts
   Bright with thy praise,
Out of my stony griefs
   Bethel I'll raise ;
So by my woes to be
‖: Nearer, my God, to thee, :‖
   Nearer to thee !

5 Or if, on joyful wing
   Cleaving the sky,
Sun, moon and stars forgot,
   Upward I fly,
Still all my song shall be,
‖: Nearer, my God, to thee, :‖
   Nearer to thee !

—Mrs. Sarah F. Adams.

NEARER THE CROSS.

151

"The cross of our Lord Jesus Christ."—Gal. 6: 14.

FANNY J. CROSBY.   MRS. J. F. KNAPP. By per.

1. "Nearer the cross!" my heart can say, I am coming near-er, Nearer the cross from day to day, I am coming near-er; Nearer the cross where Jesus died, Nearer the fountain's crimson tide, Nearer my Saviour's wounded side, I am com-ing near-er, I am coming near-er.

2. Nearer the Christian's Mercy-seat, I am coming near-er, Feasting my soul on man-na sweet, I am coming near-er; Stronger in faith, more clear I see Je-sus who gave himself for me; Nearer to him I still would be, Still I'm com-ing near-er, Still I'm coming near-er.

3. Nearer in prayer my hope aspires, I am coming near-er, Deeper the love my soul desires, I am coming near-er; Nearer the end of toil and care, Nearer the joy I long to share, Nearer the crown I soon shall wear: I am com-ing near-er, I am coming near-er.

I SHALL BE LIKE HIM.

W. A. S.
Rev. W. A. Spencer, D. D.

1. When I shall reach the more ex-cel-lent glo-ry, And all my tri-als are passed, I shall be-hold him, O won-der-ful sto-ry!
2. We shall not wait till the glo-ri-ous dawning Breaks on the vis-ion so fair, Now we may welcome the heav-en-ly morning,
3. More and more like him, re-peat the blest sto-ry, O-ver and o-ver a-gain, Changed by his spir-it from glo-ry to glo-ry,

CHORUS.

I shall be like him at last.
Now we his im-age may bear.
I shall be sat-is-fied then.

I shall be like him, I shall be like him, And in his beau-ty shall shine; I shall be like him, won-drous-ly like him, Je-sus, my Sav-iour di-vine.

Copyright, 1897, by W. A. Spencer. Used by per.

JESUS SWEETLY SAVES.—Concluded.

Je-sus sweetly saves me now, With a full, and free, an uttermost salva-tion.

WHOSOEVER WILL MAY COME.

FANNY J. CROSBY. STEPHEN C. FOSTER.

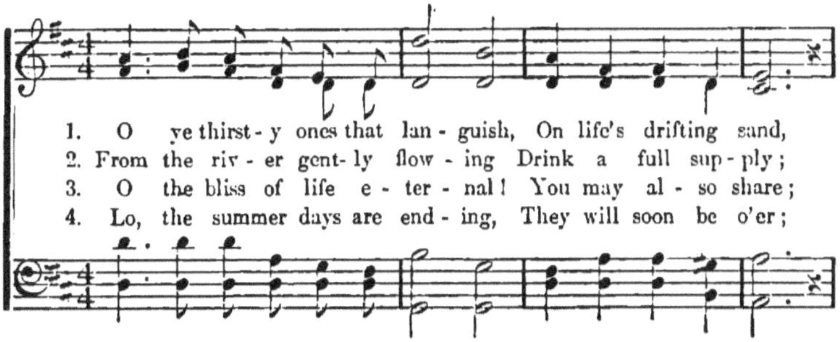

1. O ye thirst-y ones that lan-guish, On life's drifting sand,
2. From the riv-er gent-ly flow-ing Drink a full sup-ply;
3. O the bliss of life e-ter-nal! You may al-so share;
4. Lo, the summer days are end-ing, They will soon be o'er;

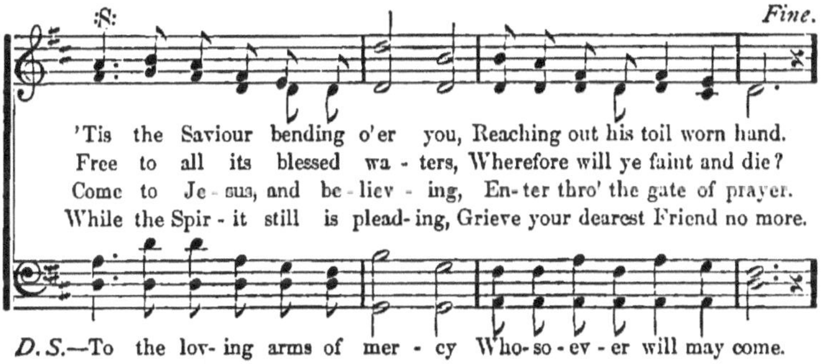

'Tis the Saviour bending o'er you, Reaching out his toil worn hand.
Free to all its blessed wa-ters, Wherefore will ye faint and die?
Come to Je-sus, and be-liev-ing, En-ter thro' the gate of prayer.
While the Spir-it still is plead-ing, Grieve your dearest Friend no more.

D.S.—To the lov-ing arms of mer-cy Who-so-ev-er will may come.

CHORUS.

Why will ye wan-der, Far a-way from home?

Copyright, 1898, by Wm. J. Kirkpatrick.

BEARING THE BANNER OF JESUS. Concluded. 157

Faith-ful till Zion's bright cit-y we see, Bearing the banner of Je-sus.
On-ward to vic-to-ry won by and by, Bearing the banner of Je-sus.
Sing-ing we march to the heav-en-ly shore, Bearing the banner of Je-sus.

D.S.—Marching we go to the dear promised land, Bearing the banner of Je-sus.

CHORUS.
Unison.

Bear-ing the ban-ner of Je-sus, Bear-ing the ban-ner of Je-sus;

LORD, I'M COMING HOME.

W. J. K. W. J. KIRKPATRICK.

With great feeling.

1. I've wan-dered far a-way from God, Now I'm com-ing home;
2. I've wast-ed ma-ny pre-cious years, Now I'm com-ing home;
3. I'm tired of sin and stray-ing, Lord, Now I'm com-ing home;
4. My soul is sick, my heart is sore, Now I'm com-ing home;

The paths of sin too long I've trod, Lord, I'm com-ing home.
I now re-pent with bit-ter tears, Lord, I'm com-ing home.
I'll trust Thy love, be-lieve Thy word, Lord, I'm com-ing home.
My strength re-new, my hope re-store, Lord, I'm com-ing home.

D. S.—O-pen wide Thine arms of love, Lord, I'm com-ing home.

CHORUS.

Com-ing home, com-ing home, Nev-er more to roam;

158. THE LIGHT OF GOD'S LOVE NEVER DIES.

LIZZIE DE ARMOND.   Mrs. J. G. WILSON.
Moderato.

1. There's a beauti- ful, death- less cit - y, That stands on eter- nity's shore;
2. The riv- er of peace thro' it floweth; The evergreen mountains of life,
3. They walk in the realms of the ransom'd, Those dear ones we cherish'd so long,

No sorrow nor sickness can en - ter, But joy fills the heart ever- more;
Like sen- tinels, stand on its bor- ders, To guard it from turmoil and strife;
Awaiting the blessed home-com- ing, "Hosanna to Christ!" is their song;

No shadows creep over the glo - ry That shines from the radiant skies,
No night full of weeping and sadness Shall hide the bright sun from our eyes,
Re- joic- ing in perfect sal- va- tion, We too in his fullness would rise,

For in that fair country of E - den, The light of God's love never dies.
For there in the glo- ry of heav- en, The light of God's love never dies.
Where thro' an e- ter- ni- ty shin- ing, The light of God's love never dies.

CHORUS.

The light of God's love never dies,......The light of God's love never dies;......
never dies;
nev- er dies,

ad lib.

For in that fair country of E - den, The light of his love never dies.

Copyright, 1899, by Mrs. J. G. Wilson.

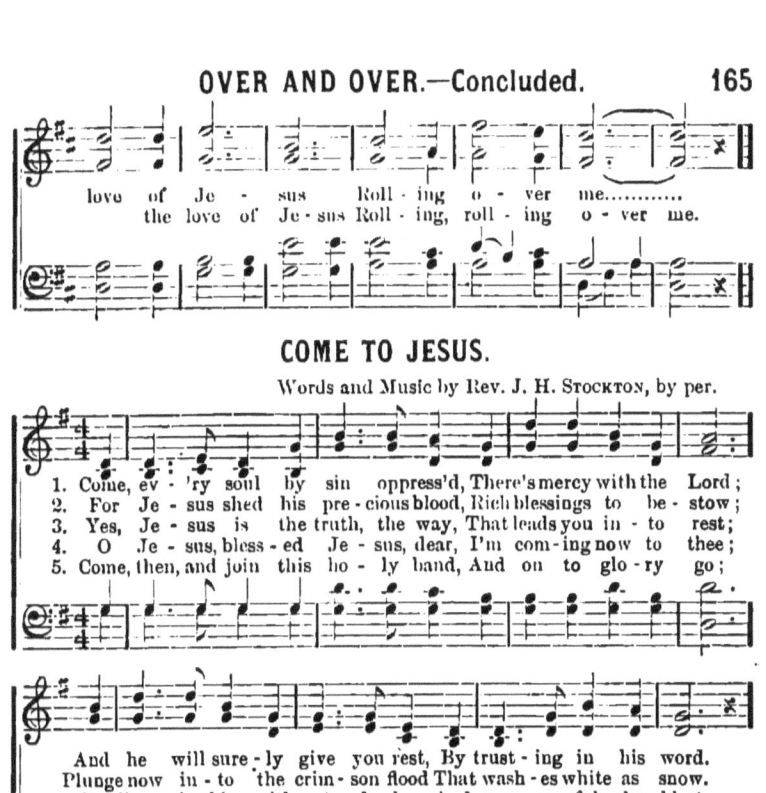

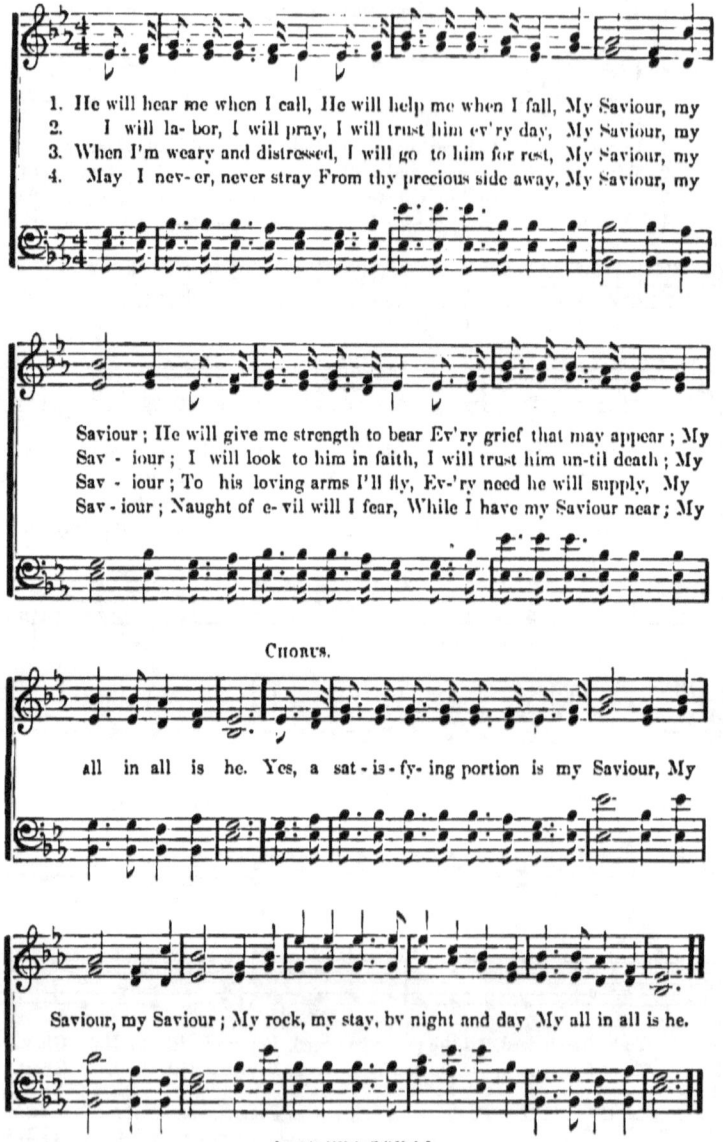

172   O 'TWAS LOVE.

A. A. PAYN.   C. AUSTIN MILES.

1. On the cross my Saviour died, Yes, for me was cru-ci-fied, Hal-le-lu-
2. From his glorious realm of light, To a world of sin-curst night, Halle-lu-

jah! hal-le-lu-jah! He endured the sin and shame, Hallelujah! Praise his
jah! hal-le-lu-jah! Jesus came my soul to save From the terrors of the

name That he should die for me.
grave; Halle-lu-jah! Praise his name.

CHORUS.

||: O 'twas love that passeth under-
Praise his name. ||: O 'twas love, 'twas love that

stand - - ing, Hal-le-lu - jah! hal-le-lu - jah! :||
passeth understanding, Hal-le-lu-jah! hal-le-lu-jah! :||

That Christ should die for me.
for me.

3. Was such love as this e'er known?
Was such love to mortals shown?
Hallelujah! hallelujah!
That my Lord his life would give
That my sinful soul might live!
Hallelujah! Praise his name.

4. This my daily song shall be,
Jesus Christ has died for me;
Hallelujah! hallelujah!
Though the waves about me roll,
They shall not o'erwhelm my soul;
Hallelujah! Praise his name.

Copyright, 1899, by Hall-Mack Co.

STILL SWEETER EVERY DAY.

W. C. Martin. C. Austin Miles.

1. To Jesus ev-'ry day I find my heart is closer drawn; He's fairer than the glo-ry of the gold and purple dawn; He's all my fan-cy pictured in its fairest dreams, and more; Each day he grows still sweeter than he was the day before.
2. His glo-ry broke upon me when I saw him from a-far; He's fairer than the lil-y, brighter than the morning star; He fills and sat-is-fies my longing spirit o'er and o'er; Each day he grows still sweeter than he was the day before.
3. My heart is sometimes heavy, but he comes with sweet relief; He folds me to his bosom when I droop with blighting grief; I love the Christ who all my burdens in his bod-y bore; Each day he grows still sweeter than he was the day before.

Chorus.

The half cannot be fan-cied this side the golden shore; O there he'll be still sweeter than he ev-er was be-fore.

The half cannot be fancied on this side the golden shore, The half cannot be fancied on this side the golden shore; O there he'll be far sweeter than he ever was before, than he ev-er was be-fore.

Copyright, 1899, by Hall-Mack Co.

LET THE SAVIOUR IN.

JOSEPHINE POLLARD.   MRS. JOSEPH F. KNAPP, by per.

Tenderly.

1. 'Tis the Sav-iour who would claim En-trance to your heart;
2. No one like the Sav-iour knocks At the sin-ner's door;
3. Oh, how can you bid him wait 'Till an-oth-er day?

Will you send your Lord a-way? Will you say, "De-part?"
'Tis no stran-ger that im-plores, He has knocked be-fore.
When al-read-y Je-sus weeps At the long de-lay

He will all your tri-als share; He will cleanse you from all sin.
He has oft-en sought your heart, Shall he cleanse it now from sin.
'Twas for you that Je-sus died, And 'tis you he longs to win.

CHORUS.

'Tis your Sav-iour, 'tis your Sav-iour standing there, Haste and
                                   let him in,

let him in, let him in, Lest he turn a-way, let him in.
                  let him in,   let him in.

I'VE BEEN REDEEMED.

W. Cowper. Arr. by Dr. T. H. Peacock, by per.

1. { There is a fountain filled with blood Drawn from Immanuel's veins,
   { And sinners plunged beneath that flood . . . . . Lose all their guilty stains.
2. { The dying thief rejoiced to see That fountain in his day,
   { And there have I, tho' vile as he, ... Washed all my sins away.

CHORUS.

I've been redeem'd, I've been redeem'd, I've been redeem'd, I've been redeem'd,
Been wash'd in the blood of the Lamb. Been redeem'd by the blood of the Lamb,
Been redeem'd by the blood of the Lamb, That flow'd on Cal-va-ry.

Glorious Fountain. Key of A.

1 There is a fountain ‖: filled with blood, :‖
   Drawn from Immanuel's veins,
   And sinners plunged ‖: beneath that
   Lose all their guilty stains. [flood, :‖
   CHO.—O, glorious fountain!
       Here will I stay,
       And in thee ever
       Wash my sins away.

2 The dying thief ‖: rejoiced to see :‖
   That fountain in his day,
   And there may I, ‖: though vile as he, :‖
   Wash all my sins away.

3 Thou dying Lamb, ‖: thy precious
   Shall never lose its power, [blood :‖
   Till all the ransomed ‖ Church of God :‖
   Are saved to sin no more.

4 E'er since by faith ‖: I saw the stream :‖
   Thy flowing wounds supply,
   Redeeming love ‖: has been my theme, :‖
   And shall be till I die.

5 Then in a nobler, ‖: sweeter song :‖
   I'll sing thy power to save,
   When this poor, lisping, ‖: stammering
   Lies silent in the grave. [tongue :‖
                                W. Cowper

O BLESSED HOPE.—Concluded. 181

THY HOLY SPIRIT, LORD, ALONE.

HENRIETTA E. BLAIR. WM. J. KIRKPATRICK.

3 Thy Holy Spirit, Lord, can bring
  The gifts we seek in prayer,
  His voice can words of comfort speak
  And still each wave of care.

4 Thy Holy Spirit, Lord, can give
  The grace we need this hour,
  And while we wait, O Spirit, come
  In sanctifying power.

Copyright, 1885, by Wm. J. Kirkpatrick.

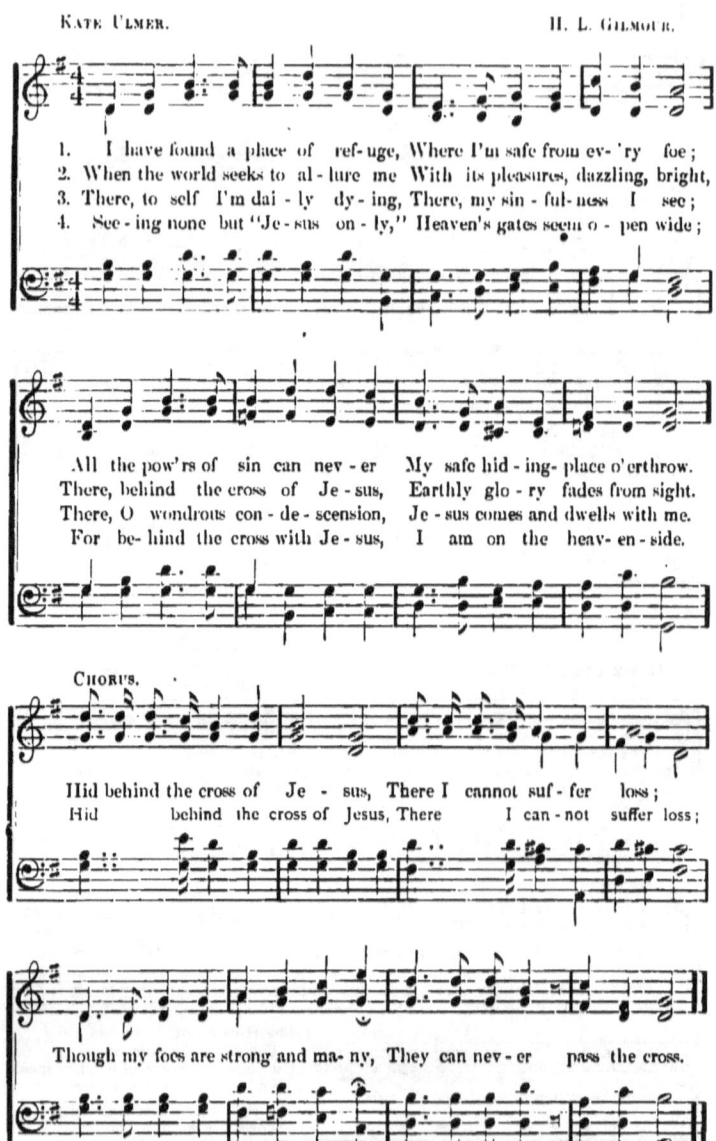

THE PLACE CALLED CALVARY.

R. E. Hewitt. Howard E. Smith.

1. O thou bleeding Lamb of God, Thou the path of death hast trod,
2. Flowing here the crimson tide, Fount of bless-ing deep and wide,
3. O the cru-el pain he bore, When the crown of thorns he wore;
4. Come, oh, come, for he'll re-ceive All who on his name be-lieve;

Pouring out thy life for me, At the place called Cal-va-ry.
Saviour, wash a-way my sin, Bring thy cleansing power with-in.
Sin-ner, come; for you and me Je-sus died on Cal-va-ry.
Find sal-va-tion full and free, At the place called Cal-va-ry.

CHORUS.

Wonderful place called Cal-va-ry, Wonderful place called Cal-va-ry;
called Cal-va-ry, called Cal-va-ry;

Love, redeem-ing love, I see, At the place called Cal-va-ry.

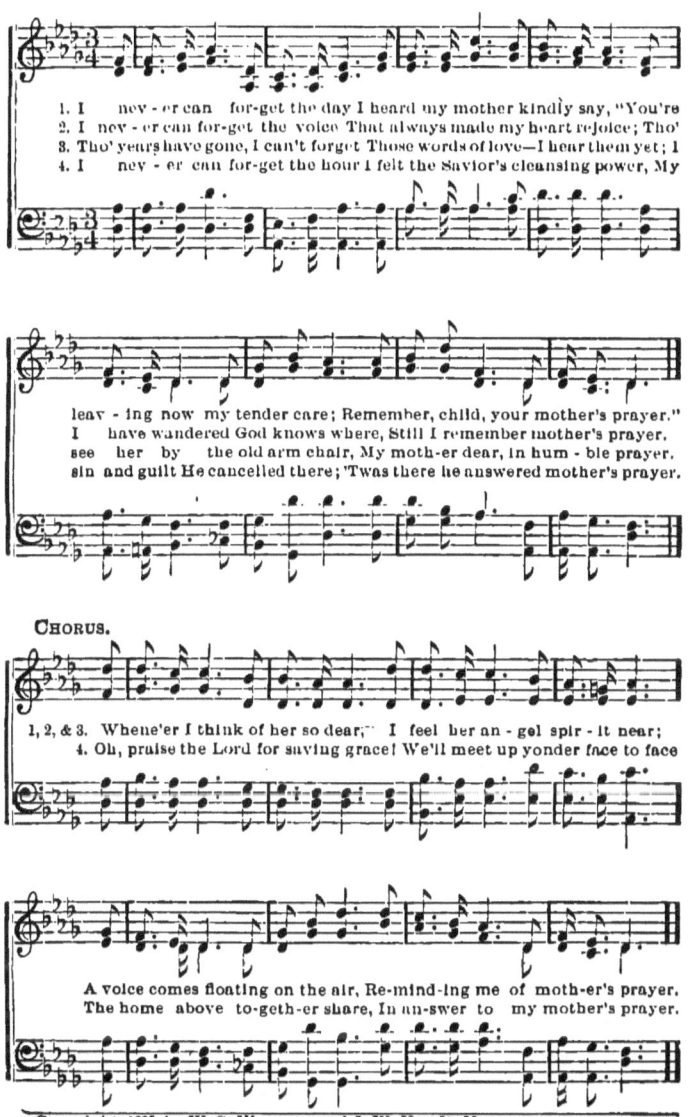

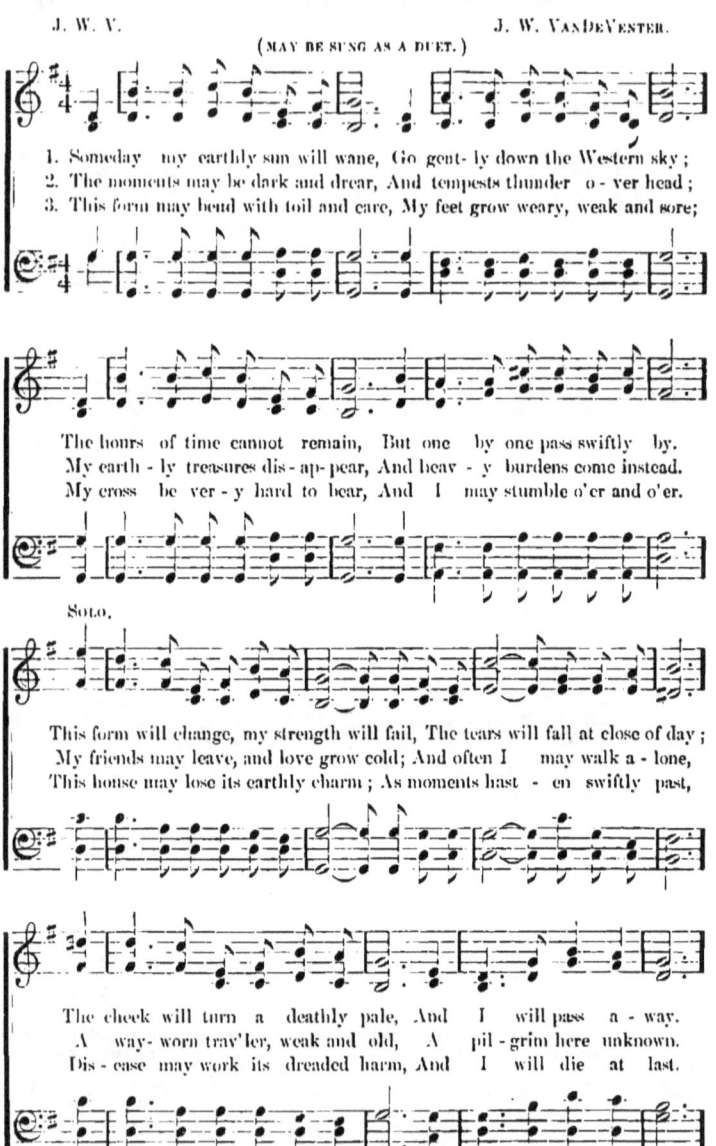

I'LL LIVE AND NE'ER GROW OLD.—Concluded.

But O the joy when I a- rise, And view the pal- a- ces of gold; I'll soar away above the skies To live and ne'er grow old.

MY SAVIOUR.

Dora Greenwell.   Wm. J. Kirkpatrick.

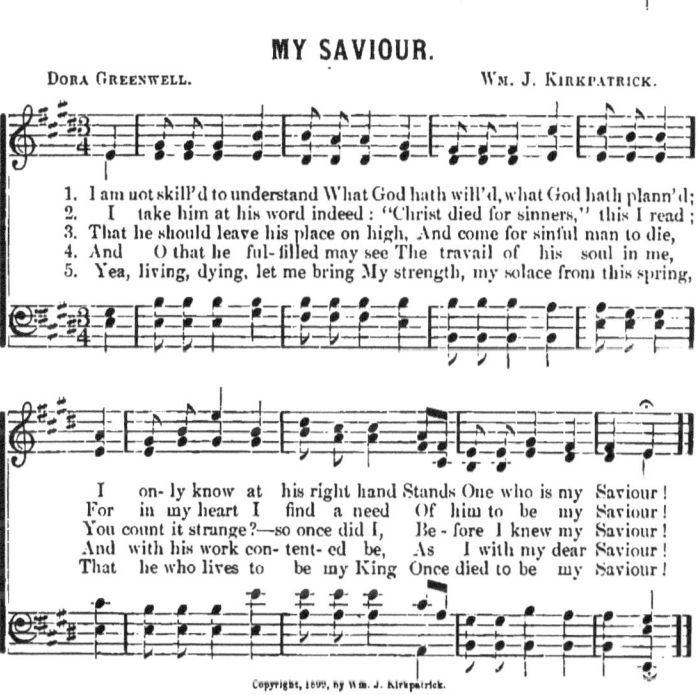

1. I am not skill'd to understand What God hath will'd, what God hath plann'd;
2. I take him at his word indeed: "Christ died for sinners," this I read;
3. That he should leave his place on high, And come for sinful man to die,
4. And O that he ful- filled may see The travail of his soul in me,
5. Yea, living, dying, let me bring My strength, my solace from this spring,

I on- ly know at his right hand Stands One who is my Saviour!
For in my heart I find a need Of him to be my Saviour!
You count it strange?—so once did I, Be- fore I knew my Saviour!
And with his work con- tent- ed be, As I with my dear Saviour!
That he who lives to be my King Once died to be my Saviour!

Copyright, 1899, by Wm. J. Kirkpatrick.

THE COMFORTER HAS COME!—Concluded.

ev-er hu-man hearts and hu-man woes a-bound; Let ev-'ry Christian
hushed the dreadful wail and fu-ry of the blast, As o'er the golden
ev-'ry cap-tive soul a full de-liv'rance brings; And thro' the va-cant
wond'ring mor-tals tell the matchless grace di-vine—That I, a child of
all the saints a-bove to all be-low re-ply, In strains of endless

D.S.—Ho-ly Ghost from heav'n, The Fa-ther's promise giv'n; Oh, spread the tidings

tongue pro-claim the joy-ful sound: The Com-fort-er has come!
hills the day ad-vanc-es fast! The Com-fort-er has come!
cells the song of tri-umph rings: The Com-fort-er has come!
hell, should in His Im-age shine! The Com-fort-er has come!
love, the song that ne'er will die: The Com-fort-er has come!

round, Wher-ev-er man is found—The Com-fort-er has come!

CHORUS. D.S.

The Com-fort-er has come, The Com-fort-er has come! The

194 FOLLOW ALL THE WAY.

GEO. W. COLLINS.   Arr. by WM. J. KIRKPATRICK.

1. I have heard my Sav-iour call-ing, I have heard my Sav-iour call-ing,
2. Tho' He leads me thro' the val-ley, Tho' He leads me thro' the val-ley,
3. Tho' He leads me thro' the gar-den, Tho' He leads me thro' the gar-den,

CHO.—Where He leads me I will fol-low, Where He leads me I will fol-low,

D.C. for Chorus.

I have heard my Saviour calling, "Take thy cross and fol-low, fol-low me."
Tho' He leads me thro' the val-ley, I'll go with Him, with Him all the way.
Tho' He leads me thro' the garden, I'll go with Him, with Him all the way.

Where He leads me I will fol-low, I'll go with Him, with Him all the way.

4 |: Tho' the path be dark and dreary, :|
I'll go with Him, with Him all the way.

5 |: Tho' He leads me to the conflict, :|
I'll go with Him, with Him all the way.

6 |: Tho' He leads through fiery trials, :|
I'll go with Him, with Him all the way.

7 |: I will follow on to know Him :|
He's my Saviour, Saviour, Brother, Friend.

8 |: He will give me grace and glory, :|
He will keep me, keep me all the way.

9 |: O 'tis sweet to follow Jesus :|
And be with Him, with Him all the way.

Copyright, 1891, by Wm. J. Kirkpatrick.

195. HE SHIELDS FROM THE STORMS OF LIFE.

E. C. MACARTNEY.   W. S. WEEDEN.

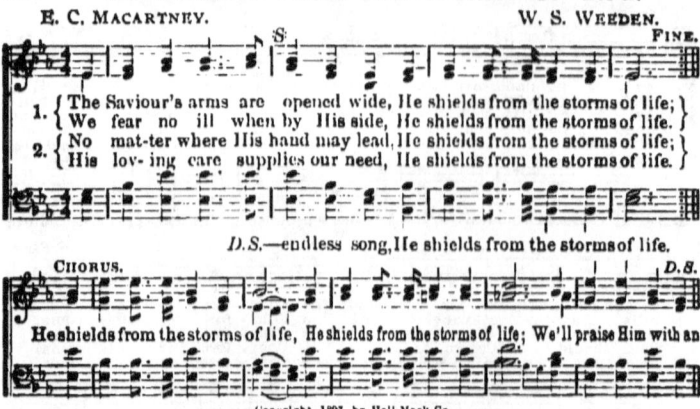

1. { The Saviour's arms are opened wide, He shields from the storms of life; \
      We fear no ill when by His side, He shields from the storms of life. }
2. { No mat-ter where His hand may lead, He shields from the storms of life; \
      His lov-ing care supplies our need, He shields from the storms of life. }

D.S.—endless song, He shields from the storms of life.

CHORUS.

He shields from the storms of life, He shields from the storms of life; We'll praise Him with an

Copyright, 1897, by Hall Mack Co.

3 Though oft our steps have gone astray,
   He shields from the storms of life;
   He brought us to the narrow way,
   He shields from the storms of life.

4 He is our loving Guide and Friend,
   He shields from the storms of life;
   He'll safely keep us to the end,
   He shields from the storms of life.

196. BLESSED BE THE NAME.

W. H. CLARK.   Arr. by WM. J. KIRKPATRICK.

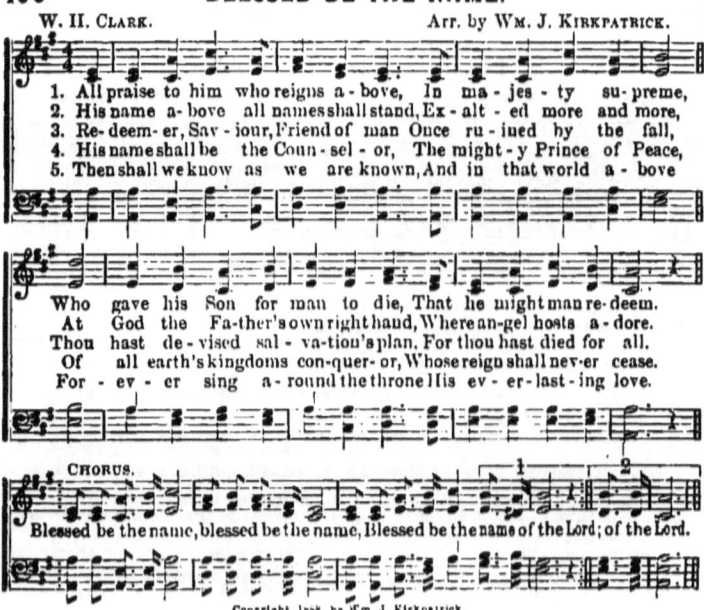

1. All praise to him who reigns a-bove, In ma-jes-ty su-preme,
2. His name a-bove all names shall stand, Ex-alt-ed more and more,
3. Re-deem-er, Sav-iour, Friend of man Once ru-ined by the fall,
4. His name shall be the Coun-sel-or, The might-y Prince of Peace,
5. Then shall we know as we are known, And in that world a-bove

Who gave his Son for man to die, That he might man re-deem.
At God the Fa-ther's own right hand, Where an-gel hosts a-dore.
Thou hast de-vised sal-va-tion's plan, For thou hast died for all.
Of all earth's kingdoms con-quer-or, Whose reign shall nev-er cease.
For-ev-er sing a-round the throne His ev-er-last-ing love.

CHORUS.

Blessed be the name, blessed be the name, Blessed be the name of the Lord; of the Lord.

Copyright, 1888, by Wm. J. Kirkpatrick.

199. THE GOSPEL FEAST.

Charles Wesley. "Come, for all things are ready." Luke 14:17.
Cho. by H. L. G. H. L. Gilmour.

1. Come, sinners, to the gospel feast; It is for you, it is for me;
   Let ev-'ry soul be Jesus' guest; It is for you, it is for me.
2. Ye need not one be left behind, It is for you, it is for me,
   For God hath bid-den all mankind, It is for you, it is for me.

D.S.—O wea-ry wand'rer, come and see, It is for you, it is for me.

Chorus.
Sal-va-tion full, sal-vation free, The price was paid on Cal-va-ry;

Copyright, 1889, by H. L. Gilmour. Used by per.

3 Sent by my Lord, on you I call ;
  The invitation is to all :

4 Come, all the world ! come, sinner, thou !
  All things in Christ are ready now.

5 Come, all ye souls by sin oppressed,
  Ye restless wanderers after rest ;

6 Ye poor, and maimed, and halt, and blind
  In Christ a hearty welcome find.

7 My message as from God receive ;
  Ye all may come to Christ and live :

8 O let this love your hearts constrain,
  Nor suffer him to die in vain.

9 See him set forth before your eyes,
  That precious, bleeding sacrifice :

10 His offered benefits embrace,
   And freely now be saved by grace.

200. STEPPING IN THE LIGHT.

L. H. Edmunds. Wm. J. Kirkpatrick.

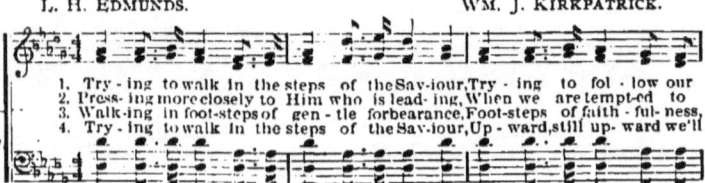

1. Try-ing to walk in the steps of the Sav-iour, Try-ing to fol-low our
2. Press-ing more closely to Him who is lead-ing, When we are tempt-ed to
3. Walk-ing in foot-steps of gen-tle forbearance, Foot-steps of faith-ful-ness,
4. Try-ing to walk in the steps of the Sav-iour, Up-ward, still up-ward we'll

Copyright, 1890, by Wm. J. Kirkpatrick.

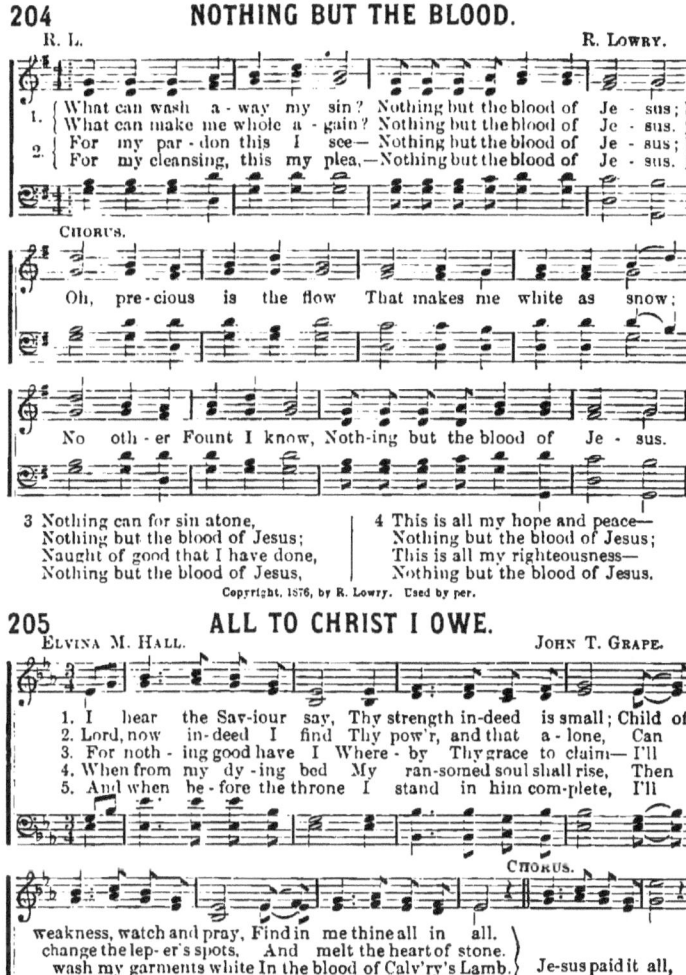

206. MY FAITH LOOKS UP TO THEE.

RAY PALMER. (OLIVET. 6s, 4s.) LOWELL MASON.

1. My faith looks up to Thee, Thou Lamb of Cal-va-ry, Sav-iour di-vine; Now hear me while I pray, Take all my guilt a-way, O let me from this day Be whol-ly thine!
2. May Thy rich grace impart Strength to my fainting heart, My zeal inspire! As Thou hast died for me, O may my love to Thee Pure, warm, and changeless be, A living fire!

3 While life's dark maze I tread,
And griefs around me spread,
Be Thou my Guide;
Bid darkness turn to day,
Wipe sorrow's tears away,
Nor let me ever stray
From Thee aside.

4 When ends life's transient dream,
When death's cold, sullen stream
Shall o'er me roll;
Blest Saviour, then, in love,
Fear and distrust remove;
O bear me safe above,
A ransomed soul!

207. MY COUNTRY! 'TIS OF THEE.

S. F. SMITH. (AMERICA. 6s, 4s.) Ad. HENRY CAREY.

1. My country! 'tis of thee, Sweet land of lib-er-ty, Of thee I sing: Land where my father's died! Land of the Pilgrim's pride! From ev'ry mountain side, Let freedom ring.
2. My na-tive country, thee, Land of the no-ble free, Thy name I love; I love thy rocks and rills, Thy woods and templed hills; My heart with rapture thrills, Like that above.
3. Let music swell the breeze, And ring from all the trees Sweet freedom's song; Let mortal tongues awake, Let all that breathe partake, Let rocks their silence break, The sound prolong.
4. Our Father's God, to Thee, Au-thor of lib-er-ty, To Thee we sing; Long may our land be bright With freedom's holy light; Pro-tect us by Thy might, Great God, our King!

208. COME, THOU ALMIGHTY KING.

C. WESLEY. (ITALIAN HYMN. 6s, 4.) FELICE GIARDINI.

1. Come, Thou al-might-y King, Help us Thy name to sing, Help us to praise; Father all-
2. Come, Thou incarnate Word, Gird on Thy mighty sword, Our pray'r attend; Come, and Thy
3. Come, ho-ly Com-fort-er, Thy sacred wit-ness bear In this glad hour: Thou who al-
4. To the great One and Three E-ter-nal prais-es be Hence—evermore! His sov'reign

COME, THOU ALMIGHTY KING. Concluded.

glo-ri-ous, O'er all vic-to-ri-ous, Come, and reign o-ver us. Ancient of Days.
people bless, And give Thy word success: Spir-it of ho-liness, On us de-scend!
might-y art, Now rule in ev-'ry heart, And ne'er from us depart, Spir-it of pow'r!
maj-es-ty May we in glo-ry see, And to e-ter-ni-ty Love and a-dore.

209   HAPPY DAY.

P. DODDRIDGE.   E. F. RIMBAULT.

1. { O hap-py day, that fixed my choice On Thee, my Saviour and my God! }
    { Well may this glowing heart re-joice, And tell its raptures all a-broad. } Hap-py
day, happy day, When Jesus wash'd my sins away! { He taught me how to watch and pray, }
    { And live re-joicing ev-'ry day. }

2 O happy bond, that seals my vows
    To Him who merits all my love!
Let cheerful anthems fill His house,
    While to that sacred shrine I move.

3 'Tis done: the great transaction's done!
    I am my Lord's, and He is mine;
He drew me, and I followed on,
    Charmed to confess the voice divine.

210   REVIVE US AGAIN.

WM. P. MACKAY.   J. J. HUSBAND.

1. We praise Thee, O God! for the Son of Thy love, For Jesus who died, and is now gone above.

CHORUS.
Hal-le-lu-jah! thine the glo-ry, Hal-le-lu-jah! A-men, Re-vive us a-gain.

2 We praise Thee, O God! for Thy Spirit of light,
    Who has shown us our Saviour, and scattered our night.
3 All glory and praise to the Lamb that was slain,
    Who has borne all our sins, and has cleansed every stain.
4 All glory and praise to the God of all grace,
    Who has bought us, and sought us, and guided our way.
5 Revive us again; fill each heart with Thy love;
    May each soul be rekindled with fire from above.

211. HOLY SPIRIT, FAITHFUL GUIDE.

M. M. W. — M. M. Wells

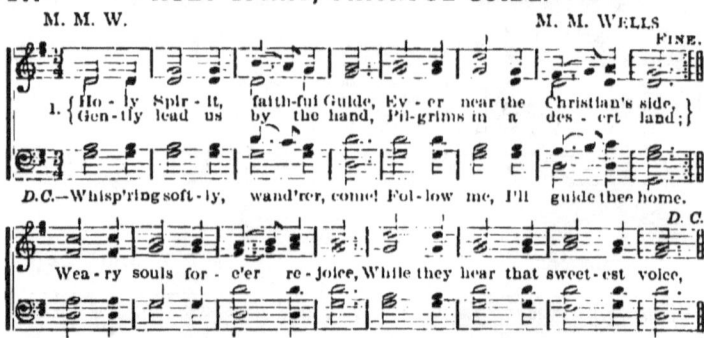

1. Holy Spirit, faithful Guide, Ever near the Christian's side,
Gently lead us by the hand, Pilgrims in a desert land;
Weary souls for e'er rejoice, While they hear that sweetest voice,
Whisp'ring softly, wand'rer, come! Follow me, I'll guide thee home.

2 Ever present, truest Friend,
Ever near, Thine aid to lend,
Leave us not to doubt and fear,
Groping on in darkness drear.
When the storms are raging sore,
Hearts grow faint, and hopes give o'er;
Whisper softly, wand'rer come!
Follow me, I'll guide thee home.

3 When our days of toil shall cease,
Waiting still for sweet release,
Nothing left but heaven and prayer,
Wond'ring if our names are there;
Wading deep the dismal flood,
Pleading naught but Jesus' blood,
Whisper softly, wand'rer, come!
Follow me, I'll guide thee home.

212. GLORY TO HIS NAME.

Rev. E. A. Hoffman. — Rev. J. H. Stockton.

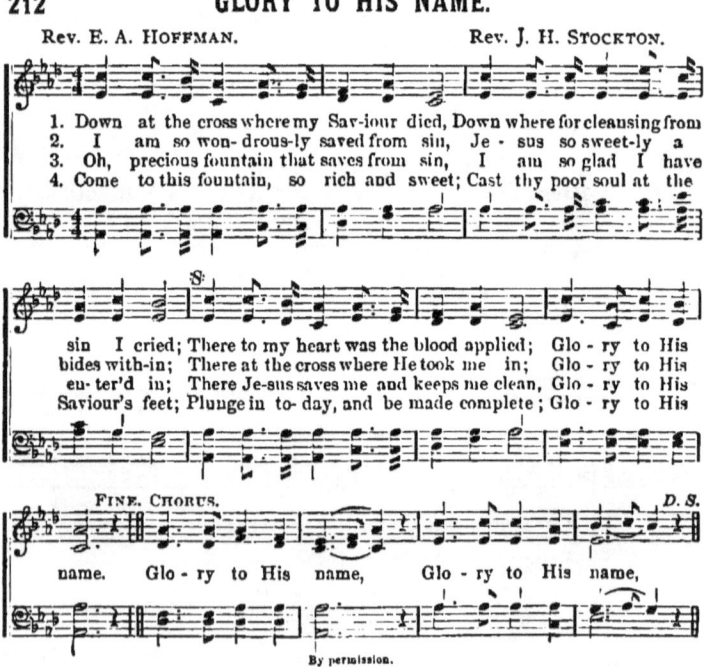

1. Down at the cross where my Saviour died, Down where for cleansing from sin I cried; There to my heart was the blood applied; Glory to His name.
2. I am so wondrously saved from sin, Jesus so sweetly abides within; There at the cross where He took me in; Glory to His name.
3. Oh, precious fountain that saves from sin, I am so glad I have entered in; There Jesus saves me and keeps me clean, Glory to His name.
4. Come to this fountain, so rich and sweet; Cast thy poor soul at the Saviour's feet; Plunge in to-day, and be made complete; Glory to His name.

CHORUS.

Glory to His name, Glory to His name,

By permission.

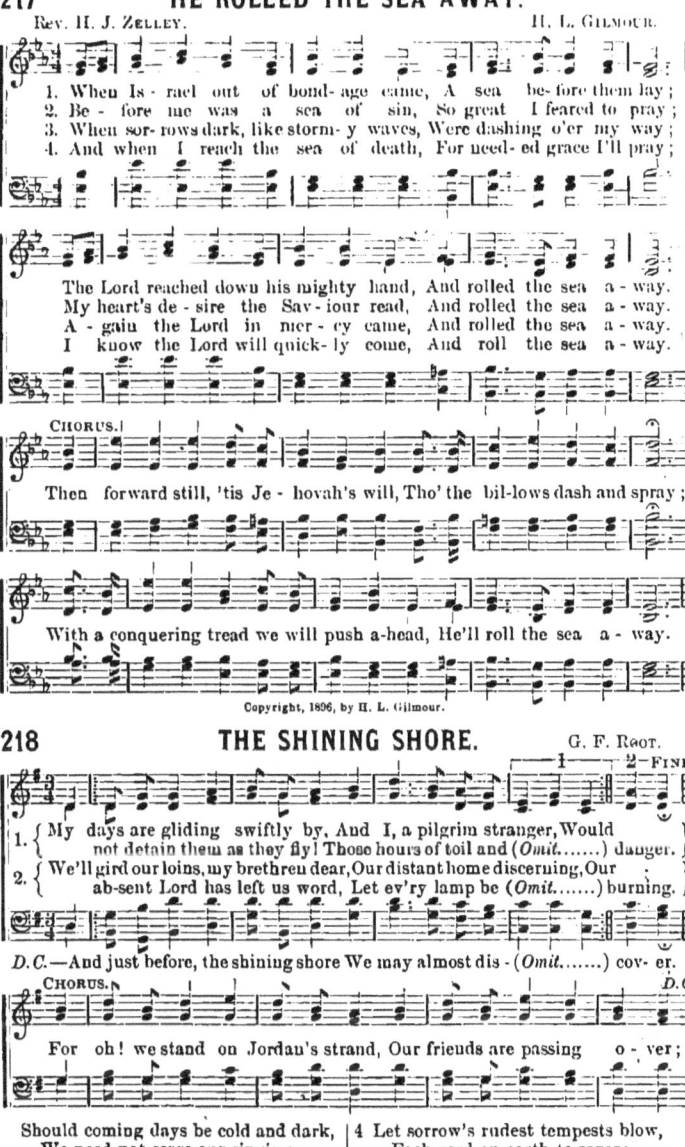

Should coming days be cold and dark,
We need not cease our singing;
That perfect rest naught can molest,
Where golden harps are ringing.

4 Let sorrow's rudest tempests blow,
Each cord on earth to sever;
Our King says, "Come," and there's our [home,
Forever, O forever!

219. 'TIS SO SWEET TO TRUST IN JESUS.

Mrs. LOUISA M. R. STEAD. WM. J. KIRKPATRICK.

1. 'Tis so sweet to trust in Je-sus, Just to take Him at His Word;
2. O, how sweet to trust in Je-sus, Just to trust His cleans-ing blood;
3. Yes, 'tis sweet to trust in Je-sus, Just from sin and self to cease;
4. I'm so glad I learn'd to trust Thee, Pre-cious Je-sus, Saviour, Friend;

Just to rest up-on His prom-ise; Just to know, "Thus saith the Lord."
Just in sim-ple faith to plunge me 'Neath the heal-ing, cleansing flood.
Just from Je-sus sim-ply tak-ing Life, and rest, and joy, and peace.
And I know that Thou art with me, Wilt be with me to the end.

CHORUS.

Je-sus, Je-sus, how I trust Him; How I've prov'd Him o'er and o'er.

Je-sus, Je-sus, Pre-cious Je-sus! O for grace to trust Him more.

Copyright, 1882, by Wm. J. Kirkpatrick.

220. CALMLY LEANING ON MY SAVIOUR.

E. E. HEWITT. WM. J. KIRKPATRICK.

1. Calm-ly lean-ing on my Sav-iour, I have peace, sweet peace,
2. Find-ing tru-est rest when wea-ry, I have peace, sweet peace,
3. Heart to heart in full com-mun-ion, I have peace, sweet peace,
4. Learn-ing more and more of Je-sus, I have peace, sweet peace,

Rest-ing in the Fa-ther's fa-vor, I have peace, sweet peace,
Joy, when else-where all is drear-y, I have peace, sweet peace,
What can break this blood-sealed un-ion? I have peace, sweet peace,
Of His sav-ing power that frees us, I have peace, sweet peace,

Copyright, 1887, by Wm. J. Kirkpatrick.

222. DEEPER YET.

Rev. Johnson Oatman, Jr. — Wm. J. Kirkpatrick.

1. In the blood from the cross I have been wash'd from sin; But to be free from dross Still I would enter in.
2. Day by day, hour by hour Blessings are sent to me; But for more of his pow'r Ever my pray'r would be.
3. Near to Christ I would live, Following him each day; What I ask he will give, So then with faith I pray.
4. Now I have peace, sweet peace, While in this world of sin; But to pray I'll not cease Till I am pure within.

CHORUS.
Deeper yet, Deeper yet, Into the crimson flood; Deeper yet, deeper yet, Under the precious blood.

Copyright, 1896, by Wm. J. Kirkpatrick.

223. NEARER, STILL NEARER.

C. H. M. — Mrs. C. H. Morris.

1. Nearer, still nearer, close to thy heart, Draw me, my Saviour, so precious thou art; Fold me, O fold me close to thy breast, Shelter me
2. Nearer, still nearer, nothing I bring, Naught as an off'ring to Jesus my King; Only my sinful, now contrite heart, Grant me the
3. Nearer, still nearer, Lord, to be thine Sin, with its follies, I gladly resign; All of its pleasures, pomp and its pride, Give me but
4. Nearer, still nearer, while life shall last, Till all its struggles and trials are past; Then thro' eternity, ever I'll be Nearer, my

Copyright, 1896, by H. L. Gilmour.

NEARER, STILL NEARER.—Concluded.

safe in that "Haven of Rest," Shelter me safe in that "Haven of Rest."
cleansing thy blood doth impart, Grant me the cleansing thy blood doth impart.
Je - sus, my Lord cruci- fied, Give me but Je- sus, my Lord cruci- fied.
Saviour, still near- er to thee, Nearer, my Saviour, still nearer to thee.

224 J. W. VanDeVenter.   I SURRENDER ALL.   W. S. Weeden.

Solo.

1. All to Je-sus I sur-ren-der, All to him I free-ly give;
   I will ev-er love and trust him, In his presence dai-ly live.
2. All to Je-sus I sur-ren-der, Humbly at his feet I bow;
   Worldly pleasures all for-sak-en, Take me, Je-sus, take me now.
3. All to Je-sus I sur-ren-der, Make me, Saviour, whol-ly thine;
   Let me feel the Ho-ly Spir-it, Tru-ly know that thou art mine.

Chorus.

I sur-ren-der all, I sur-ren-der all ;
I surrender all, I surrender all ;
All to thee, my bless-ed Sav-iour, I sur-ren-der all.

4 All to Jesus I surrender,
  Lord, I give myself to thee;
  Fill me with thy love and power,
  Let thy blessing fall on me.

5 All to Jesus I surrender,
  Now I feel the sacred flame;
  O the joy of full salvation!
  Glory, glory to his name!

Copyright, 1896, by Weeden & VanDeVenter.

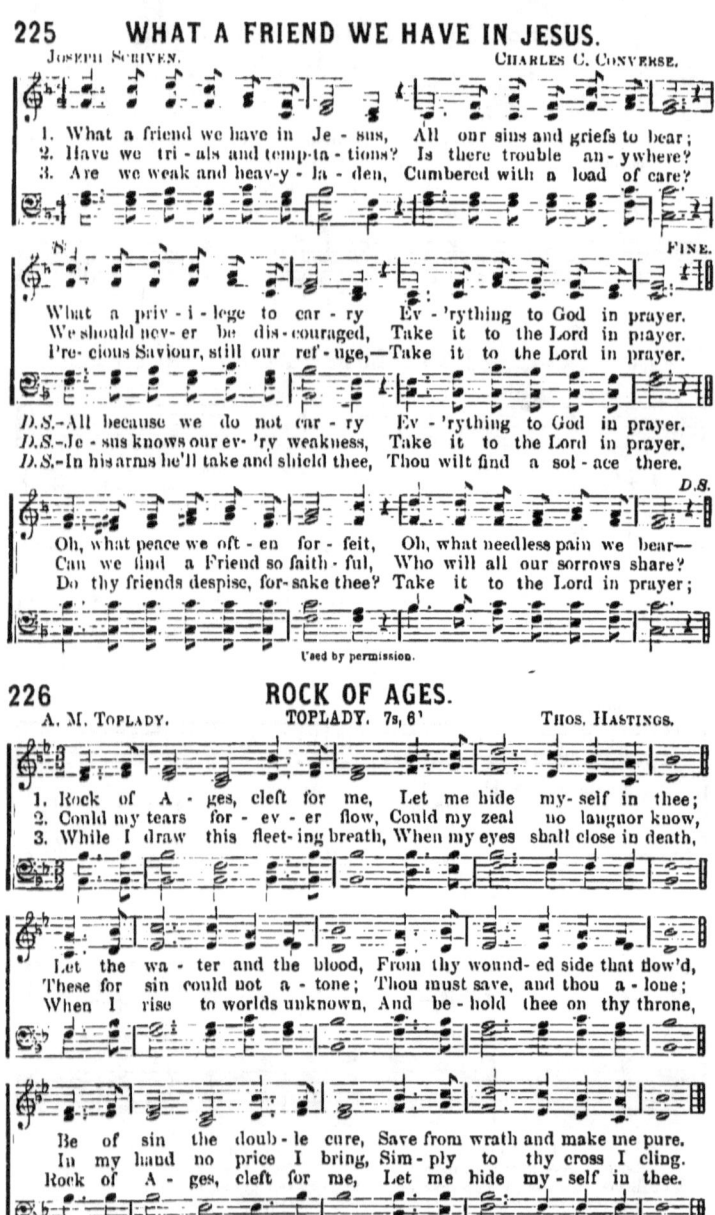

227 O JESUS, THOU ART STANDING.

ST. HILDA. 7s. 6s. D.

Wm. W. How.   Justin H. Knight, et. al.

1. O Jesus, thou art standing Outside the fast-closed door, In lowly patience waiting To pass the threshold o'er: We bear the name of Christians His name and sign we bear: Oh, shame, thrice shame upon us! To keep him standing there.
2. O Jesus, thou art knocking: And lo! that hand is scarred, And thorns thy brow encircle, And tears thy face have marred, Oh, love that passeth knowledge, So patiently to wait! Oh, sin that hath no equal, So fast to bar the gate!
3. O Jesus, thou art pleading In accents meek and low, "I died for you, my children, And will ye treat me so?" O Lord, with shame and sorrow We open now the door: Dear Saviour, enter, enter, And leave us nevermore!

228   JESUS, LOVER OF MY SOUL.

Charles Wesley.   S. B. Marsh.

1. Jesus, lover of my soul, Let me to thy bosom fly,
While the nearer waters roll, While the tempest still is high!
Hide me, O my Saviour, hide, Till the storm of life is past;
D.C.—Safe into the haven guide, Oh, receive my soul at last.

2 Other refuge have I none,
  Hangs my helpless soul on thee ;
Leave, oh leave me not alone,
  Still support and comfort me.
All my trust on thee is stayed,
  All my help from thee I bring ;
Cover my defenseless head.
  With the shadow of thy wing.

3 Thou, O Christ, art all I want ;
  More than all in thee I find ;
Raise the fallen! cheer the faint!
  Heal the sick ! and lead the blind !
Just and holy is thy name,
  I am all unrighteousness :
Vile and full of sin I am,
  Thou art full of truth and grace.

229. FROM GREENLAND'S ICY MOUNTAINS.

Heber. MISSIONARY HYMN. 7s, 6s. **Mason.**

1. From Greenland's i-cy mountains, From In-dia's cor-al strand;
Where Af-ric's sun-ny fountains, (Omit.................)
Roll down their golden sand; From many an ancient riv-er, From many a palm-y plain, They call us to de-liv-er, Their land from er-ror's chain.

2 Shall we, whose souls are lighted,
   With wisdom from on high,
Shall we, to men benighted,
   The lamp of life deny?
Salvation!—O salvation!
   The joyful sound proclaim,
Till earth's remotest nation
   Has learned Messiah's name.

3 Waft, waft, ye winds, his story,
   And you, ye waters, roll,
Till, like a sea of glory,
   It spreads from pole to pole;
Till o'er our ransomed nature,
   The Lamb for sinners slain,
Redeemer, King, Creator,
   In bliss returns to reign.

230. COME, YE DISCONSOLATE.

Thos. Moore. **Samuel Webbe.**

1. Come, ye dis-con-so-late! wher-e'er ye lan-guish, Come to the mer-cy-seat, fer-vent-ly kneel: Here bring your wounded hearts, Here tell your anguish; Earth has no sor-row that heav'n cannot heal.
2. Joy of the des-o-late! light of the stray-ing, Hope of the pen-i-tent, fade-less and pure! Here speaks the Com-fort-er, Ten-der-ly say-ing, Earth has no sor-row that heav'n cannot cure.
3. Here see the bread of life; see wa-ters flow-ing, Forth from the throne of God, pure from a-bove; Come to the feast of love; Come, ev-er knowing, Earth has no sor-rows but heav'n can re-move.

231. STEP OUT ON THE PROMISE.

MAGGIE POTTER. Arr. by E. F. M.   E. F. MILLER.

1. O mourner in Zion, how blessed art thou, For Jesus is waiting to comfort thee now, Fear not to rely on the word of thy God; Step out on the promise,—get under the blood.
2. O ye that are hungry and thirsty, rejoice! For ye shall be filled; do you hear that sweet voice Inviting you now to the banquet of God? Step out on the promise,—get under the blood.
3. Who sighs for a heart from iniquity free? O poor, troubled soul! there's a promise for thee, There's rest, weary one, in the bosom of God; Step out on the promise,—get under the blood.
4. Step out on the promise, and Christ you shall win, "The blood of his Son cleanseth us from all sin," It cleanseth me now, hallelujah to God! I rest on his promise,—I'm under the blood.

From "The Shout of Victory." By per.

232. EVENTIDE. 10s.

HENRY F. LYTE.   WILLIAM HENRY MONK.

1. Abide with me; fast falls the eventide; The darkness deepens; Lord, with me abide! When other helpers fail, and comforts flee, Help of the helpless, O abide with me!
2. Swift to its close ebbs out life's little day; Earth's joys grow dim, its glories pass away; Change and decay in all around I see; O thou, who changest not, abide with me!
3. I need thy presence ev'ry passing hour; What but thy grace can foil the tempter's pow'r? Who, like thyself, my guide and stay can be? Thro' cloud and sunshine, Lord, abide with me!
4. I fear no foe, with thee at hand to bless; Ills have no weight, and tears no bitterness; Where is death's sting? where, grave, thy victory? I triumph still, if thou abide with me!

238. CORONATION. C. M.

E. PERRONET.   OLIVER HOLDEN.

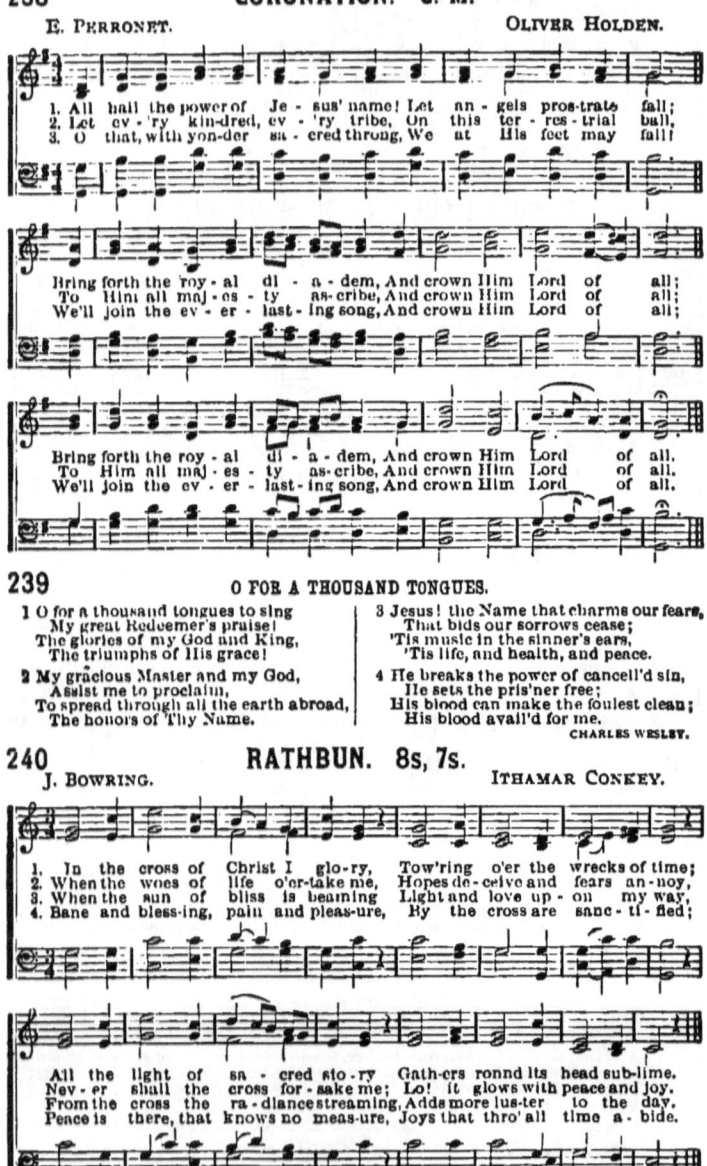

1. All hail the power of Jesus' name! Let angels prostrate fall;
Bring forth the royal diadem, And crown Him Lord of all;
Bring forth the royal diadem, And crown Him Lord of all.

2. Let ev'ry kindred, ev'ry tribe, On this terrestrial ball,
To Him all majesty ascribe, And crown Him Lord of all;
To Him all majesty ascribe, And crown Him Lord of all.

3. O that, with yonder sacred throng, We at His feet may fall!
We'll join the everlasting song, And crown Him Lord of all;
We'll join the everlasting song, And crown Him Lord of all.

239. O FOR A THOUSAND TONGUES.

1 O for a thousand tongues to sing
My great Redeemer's praise!
The glories of my God and King,
The triumphs of His grace!

2 My gracious Master and my God,
Assist me to proclaim,
To spread through all the earth abroad,
The honors of Thy Name.

3 Jesus! the Name that charms our fears,
That bids our sorrows cease;
'Tis music in the sinner's ears,
'Tis life, and health, and peace.

4 He breaks the power of cancell'd sin,
He sets the pris'ner free;
His blood can make the foulest clean;
His blood avail'd for me.

CHARLES WESLEY.

240. RATHBUN. 8s, 7s.

J. BOWRING.   ITHAMAR CONKEY.

1. In the cross of Christ I glory, Tow'ring o'er the wrecks of time;
All the light of sacred story Gathers round its head sublime.

2. When the woes of life o'ertake me, Hopes deceive and fears annoy,
Never shall the cross forsake me; Lo! it glows with peace and joy.

3. When the sun of bliss is beaming Light and love upon my way,
From the cross the radiance streaming, Adds more luster to the day.

4. Bane and blessing, pain and pleasure, By the cross are sanctified;
Peace is there, that knows no measure, Joys that thro' all time abide.

DENNIS. S. M.

ALBERT MIDLANE.   H. G. NÄGELI.

1. Re-vive thy work, O Lord, Thy might-y arm make bare;
2. Re-vive thy work, O Lord, Cre-ate soul-thirst for Thee;
3. Re-vive thy work, O Lord, Ex-alt Thy pre-cious name;

Speak with the voice that wakes the dead, And make thy peo-ple hear.
And hung'ring for the Bread of Life, O may our spir-its be!
And by the Ho-ly Ghost, our love For Thee and Thine in-flame.

242 BLEST BE THE TIE. S. M.

1 Blest be the tie that binds
  Our hearts in Christian love:
The fellowship of kindred minds
  Is like to that above.

2 Before our Father's throne
  We pour our ardent prayers;
Our fears, our hopes, our aims are one,
  Our comforts and our cares.

3 We share our mutual woes,
  Our mutual burdens bear;
And often for each other flows
  The sympathizing tear.

4 When we asunder part,
  It gives us inward pain;
But we shall still be joined in heart,
  And hope to meet again.
        JOHN FAWCETT.

243 A CHARGE TO KEEP. S. M.

1 A charge to keep I have,
  A God to glorify;
A never-dying soul to save,
  And fit it for the sky.

2 To serve the present age,
  My calling to fulfill,
O may it all my powers engage,
  To do my Master's will!

3 Arm me with jealous care,
  As in Thy sight to live;
And O, thy servant, Lord, prepare
  A strict account to give!

4 Help me to watch and pray,
  And on thyself rely,
Assured, if I my trust betray,
  I shall forever die.
        CHAS. WESLEY.

BOYLSTON. S. M.

LOWELL MASON.

244 AND CAN I YET DELAY. S. M.

1 And can I yet delay
  My little all to give?
To tear my soul from earth away
  For Jesus to receive?

2 Nay, but I yield, I yield!
  I can hold out no more:
I sink, by dying love compelled,
  And own Thee conqueror!

3 Though late, I all forsake;
  My friends, my all resign:
Gracious Redeemer, take, O take,
  And seal me ever Thine.

4 Come, and possess me whole,
  Nor hence again remove:
Settle and fix my wav'ring soul
  With all thy weight of love.
        CHAS. WESLEY.

245 EVILS OF INTEMPERANCE. S. M.

1 Mourn for the thousands slain,
  The youthful and the strong;
Mourn for the wine cup's fearful reign,
  And the deluded throng.

2 Mourn for the ruined soul—
  Eternal life and light
Lost by the fiery, maddening bowl,
  And turned to hopeless night.

3 Mourn for the lost;—but call,
  Call to the strong, the free;
Rouse them to shun that dreadful fall,
  And to the refuge flee.

4 Mourn for the lost;—but pray,
  Pray to our God above,
To break the fell destroyer's sway,
  And show His saving love.

DUKE ST. L. M.

ISAAC WATTS. JOHN HATTON.

1. From all that dwell be-low the skies, Let the Cre-a-tor's praise a-rise;
2. E-ter-nal are Thy mer-cies, Lord; E-ter-nal truth at-tends Thy word;

Let the Re-deem-er's name be sung Thro' ev'ry land, by ev'ry tongue.
Thy praise shall sound from shore to shore Till suns shall rise and set no more.

247 JESUS SHALL REIGN. L. M.

1 Jesus shall reign where'er the sun
   Does his successive journeys run;
   His kingdom stretch from shore to shore,
   Till moons shall wax and wane no more.

2 From north to south the princes meet
   To pay their homage at His feet;
   While western empires own their Lord,
   And savage tribes attend His word.

3 To Him shall endless prayer be made,
   And endless praises crown His head;
   His name, like sweet perfume, shall rise
   With every morning sacrifice.

4 People and realms, of every tongue,
   Dwell on His love with sweetest song,
   And infant voices shall proclaim
   Their early blessings on His name.
   ISAAC WATTS.

248 GLORYING IN THE CROSS. L. M.

1 When I survey the wondrous cross
   On which the Prince of glory died,
   My richest gain I count but loss,
   And pour contempt on all my pride.

2 Forbid it, Lord, that I should boast,
   Save in the death of Christ, my God;
   All the vain things that charm me most,
   I sacrifice them to His blood.

3 See, from His head, His hands, His feet,
   Sorrow and love flow mingled down!
   Did e'er such love and sorrow meet?
   Or thorns compose so rich a crown?

4 Were the whole realm of nature mine,
   That were a present far too small;
   Love so amazing, so divine,
   Demands my soul, my life, my all.
   ISAAC WATTS.

HAMBURG. L. M.

Arr. by LOWELL MASON.

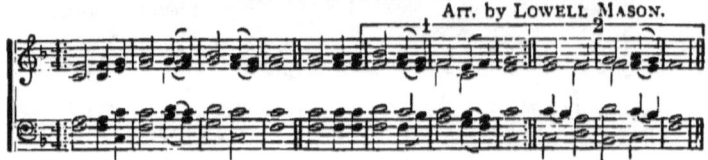

249 LORD, I AM THINE. L. M.

1 Lord, I am Thine, entirely Thine,
   Purchased and saved by blood divine;
   With full consent Thine would I be,
   And own Thy sovereign right in me.

2 Thine would I live, Thine would I die,
   Be Thine through all eternity;
   The vow is past, beyond repeal,
   Now will I set the solemn seal.

3 Here, at that cross where flows the blood
   That bought my guilty soul for God,
   Thee, my new Master, now I call,
   And consecrate to Thee my all.

4 Do Thou assist a feeble worm
   The great engagement to perform;
   Thy grace can full assistance lend,
   And on that grace I dare depend.
   SAMUEL DAVIES.

250 NOT ASHAMED OF JESUS. L. M.

1 Jesus! and shall it ever be,
   A mortal man ashamed of Thee?
   Ashamed of Thee, whom angels praise,
   Whose glories shine thro' endless days?

2 Ashamed of Jesus! sooner far
   Let evening blush to own a star;
   He sheds the beams of light divine
   O'er this benighted soul of mine.

3 Ashamed of Jesus! just as soon
   Let midnight be ashamed of noon:
   'Tis midnight with my soul till He,
   Bright Morning Star, bid darkness flee.

4 Ashamed of Jesus! that dear Friend,
   On whom my hopes of heaven depend?
   No; when I blush, be this my shame,
   That I no more revere His name.
   JOSEPH GRIGG.

ARLINGTON. C. M.

CHARLES WESLEY.   THOMAS A. ARNE.

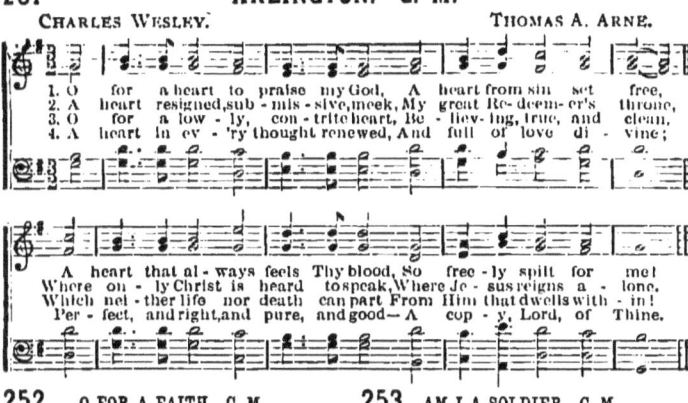

1. O for a heart to praise my God, A heart from sin set free,
A heart that al-ways feels Thy blood, So free-ly spilt for me!
2. A heart resigned, sub-mis-sive, meek, My great Re-deem-er's throne,
Where on-ly Christ is heard to speak, Where Je-sus reigns a-lone.
3. O for a low-ly, con-trite heart, Be-liev-ing, true, and clean,
Which nei-ther life nor death can part From Him that dwells with-in!
4. A heart in ev-'ry thought renewed, And full of love di-vine;
Per-fect, and right, and pure, and good—A cop-y, Lord, of Thine.

252   O FOR A FAITH. C. M.

1 O for a faith that will not shrink,
   Though pressed by ev'ry foe,
That will not tremble on the brink
   Of any earthly woe!

2 That will not murmur nor complain
   Beneath the chastening rod,
But, in the hour of grief or pain,
   Will lean upon its God;

3 A faith that shines more bright and clear
   When tempests rage without;
That when in danger knows no fear,
   In darkness feels no doubt;

4 Lord, give us such a faith as this;
   And then, whate'er may come,
We'll taste, e'en here, the hallowed bliss
   Of an eternal home.

            WILLIAM HILEY BATHURST.

253   AM I A SOLDIER. C. M.

1 Am I a soldier of the cross,
   A foll'wer of the Lamb,
And shall I fear to own His cause,
   Or blush to speak His name?

2 Must I be carried to the skies
   On flowery beds of ease,
While others fought to win the prize,
   And sailed through bloody seas?

3 Are there no foes for me to face?
   Must I not stem the flood?
Is this vile world a friend to grace,
   To help me on to God?

4 Sure I must fight if I would reign;
   Increase my courage, Lord;
I'll bear the toil, endure the pain,
   Supported by Thy word.

            ISAAC WATTS.

AZMON. C. M.

C. G. GLASER.

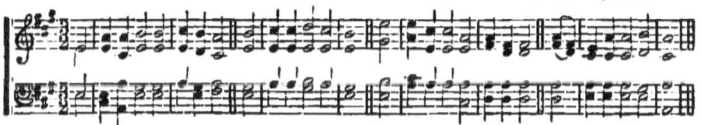

254   FOREVER HERE MY REST. C. M.

1 Forever here my rest shall be,
   Close to Thy bleeding side;
This all my hope, and all my plea,
   For me the Saviour died.

2 My dying Saviour and my God,
   Fountain for guilt and sin,
Sprinkle me ever with Thy blood,
   And cleanse and keep me clean.

3 Wash me, and make me thus Thine own;
   Wash me, and mine Thou art;
Wash me, but not my feet alone,—
   My hands, my head, my heart.

4 Th' atonement of Thy blood apply,
   Till faith to sight improve;
Till hope in full fruition die,
   And all my soul be love.

            CHARLES WESLEY.

255   THE DEAREST NAME. C. M.

1 How sweet the name of Jesus sounds
   In a believer's ear!
It soothes his sorrows, heals his wounds,
   And drives away his fear.

2 It makes the wounded spirit whole,
   And calms the troubled breast;
'Tis manna to the hungry soul,
   And to the weary, rest.

3 Dear Name, the rock on which I build,
   My shield and hiding-place;
My never-failing treasury, filled
   With boundless stores of grace.

4 Jesus, my Shepherd, Saviour, Friend,
   My Prophet, Priest, and King;
My Lord, my Life, my Way, my End,
   Accept the praise I bring!

            JOHN NEWTON.

NETTLETON. 8s, 7s. D.

JOHN WYETH.

256 COME THOU FOUNT.

1 Come, Thou Fount of every blessing,
  Tune my heart to sing Thy grace;
 Streams of mercy, never ceasing,
  Call for songs of loudest praise.
 Teach me some melodious sonnet,
  Sung by flaming tongues above;
 Praise the mount, I'm fixed upon it,
  Mount of Thy redeeming love!

2 Here I'll raise mine Ebenezer,
  Hither, by Thy help, I'm come;
 And I hope, by Thy good pleasure,
  Safely to arrive at home.
 Jesus sought me, when a stranger,
  Wand'ring from the fold of God;
 He, to rescue me from danger,
  Interposed His precious blood!

3 O! to grace how great a debtor,
  Daily I'm constrained to be!
 Let Thy goodness, like a fetter,
  Bind my wand'ring heart to Thee!
 Prone to wander, Lord, I feel it,
  Prone to leave the God I love;
 Here's my heart, O take and seal it!
  Seal it for Thy courts above.

R. ROBINSON.

257 JESUS, I MY CROSS.

1 Jesus, I my cross have taken,
  All to leave, and follow thee;
 Naked, poor, despised, forsaken,
  Thou, from hence, my all shalt be:
 Perish every fond ambition,
  All I've sought, and hoped, and known;
 Yet how rich is my condition,
  God and heaven are still my own!

2 Man may trouble and distress me,
  'Twill but drive me to thy breast;
 Life with trials hard may press me,
  Heaven will bring me sweeter rest.
 O 'tis not in grief to harm me,
  While thy love is left to me;
 O 'twere not in joy to charm me,
  Were that joy unmixed with thee.

3 Haste thee on from grace to glory,
  Armed by faith, and winged by prayer;
 Heaven's eternal day's before thee,
  God's own hand shall guide thee there.
 Soon shall close thy earthly mission,
  Swift shall pass thy pilgrim days,
 Hope shall change to glad fruition,
  Faith to sight, and prayer to praise.

HENRY F. LYTE.

GREENVILLE. 8s, 7s. D.

J. T. ROSSEAU.

258 COME, YE SINNERS.

1 Come, ye sinners, poor and needy,
  Weak and wounded, sick and sore;
 Jesus ready stands to save you,
  Full of pity, love, and power:
   He is able,
  He is willing, doubt no more.

2 Now, ye needy, come and welcome,
  God's free bounty glorify;
 True belief and true repentance,
  Every grace that brings you nigh,
   Without money,
  Come to Jesus Christ and buy.

3 Let not conscience make you linger,
  Nor of fitness fondly dream;
 All the fitness he requireth
  Is to feel your need of Him:
   This He gives you;
  'Tis the Spirit's glimm'ring beam.

4 Come, ye weary, heavy laden,
  Bruised and mangled by the fall;
 If you tarry till you're better,
  You will never come at all;
   Not the righteous,
  Sinners, Jesus came to call.

JOSEPH HART.

259 THE PILGRIM'S GUIDE.

1 Guide me, O Thou great Jehovah,
  Pilgrim through this barren land;
 I am weak, but Thou art mighty;
  Hold me with Thy powerful hand:
   Bread of heaven,
  Feed me till I want no more.

2 Open, now, the crystal fountain,
  Whence the healing waters flow;
 Let the fiery, cloudy pillar
  Lead me all my journey through;
   Strong Deliv'rer,
  Be Thou still my strength and shield.

3 When I tread the verge of Jordan,
  Bid my anxious fears subside;
 Bear me through the swelling current;
  Land me safe on Canaan's side:
   Songs of praises
  I will ever give to Thee.

WILLIAM WILLIAMS.

TOPICAL INDEX.

Acceptance, 157, 163, 179, 237.
Apostles' Creed, 3.
Aspiration, 64, 115, 147, 206, 223, 251.
Assurance, 16, 35, 52, 98, 102, 153, 184, 192, 236.
Atonement, 11, 55, 177, 248, 254.
Christian Counsel, 33, 84, 93, 98, 107, 143, 204, 221, 222.
Christian Encouragement, 5, 12, 31, 48, 52, 83, 89, 93, 103.
Christian Experience, 11, 35, 72, 92, 113, 140, 144, 149, 154, 164, 175, 178, 182, 184, 212.
Christian Fellowship, 116, 242.
Cleansing, 87, 221, 236, 254.
Commandments, 3.
Consecration, 17, 38, 43, 152, 161, 221, 222, 224, 233, 244, 249.
Cross, 106, 151, 182, 212, 240, 248.
Devotion, 15, 43, 63, 133, 150, 188, 251, 260.
Entreaty, 10, 33, 62, 73, 136, 166, 176.
Evening, 198, 232, 235.
Faith and Trust, 74, 110, 116, 125, 141, 142, 149, 150, 197, 102, 206, 217, 219, 252.
Fellowship with Jesus, 64, 110, 121, 128, 171.
Future, 14, 16, 19, 28, 57, 95, 119, 168, 173, 180, 190.
Gospel, provisions of, 123, 199, 215.
  Fountain, 66, 177.
  Living Waters, 72, 87.
  Winning its way, 104.
Grace, 30, 201, 256.
Guidance, 174, 250.
Heaven, 6, 25, 32, 61, 158, 190, 218.
  A light on the other side, 90.
  Anticipated, 14, 28, 89, 126, 127, 173, 190.
  Beautiful city, 160, 168.
  Coronation day, 95.
  I'll be there, 203.
  Is my home, 202.
  Journey to, 10, 86, 107, 127, 39.
  Looking this way, 75.
  No stranger there, 185.
  Sweet land of bliss, 120.
  When the roll is called, 159.
Holy Spirit (Comforter), 70, 84, 97, 158, 169, 181, 193, 211, 216.
Hope, 142, 180.
Invitation, 10, 20, 62, 118, 122, 129, 143, 155, 165, 166, 167, 199, 205, 214, 230, 237, 258.
Jesus, Able to save, 46.
  All in all, 96.
  A gift of love, 26.
  Bearing burdens, 7, 94.
  Blood of, 16, 69, 82, 204, 231.
  Calling, 118, 167.
  Following, 21, 161, 122, 194, 200.
  Friend, 41, 129, 225.
  He's the one, 68.
  I love thee, 213.
  I shall be like Him, 153.
  Is near, 99.
  Kind is the heart of, 59.
  Knows it all, 103.
  Leaning on, 171, 220.
  Let Him have His way, 17.
  Looking for me, 138.
  Lover of my soul, 228.
  Name of, 255.
  Never leave nor forsake, 101, 137.
  Not ashamed of, 132, 250.
  On lone calvary, 55.
  Only, 7, 8.
  Paid it all, 205, 26.
  Rock of Ages, 220.
  Satisfying portion, 170.
  Saves, 15, 113, 178.
  Saviour, 33, 65, 191.
  Seeking to save, 77.
  Shepherd, 77, 100.
  Standing and knocking, 62, 176, 227.
  Sufficient for me, 144.
  Walk with us to-day, 128.
  When He comes, 13, 95, 126.
  Who is this, 54.
  Will bid me welcome, 135.
  Upheld by the power of, 105.
Judgment day, 16, 57, 95.
Light of the Gospel, 104.
  Into the marvelous, 73.
  On the other side, 90.
  Of God's love, never, 88.
  Stepping in the, 200.
  Walking in the, 27, 81.
Love, 112, 142, 213.
  Arrow of love, 49.
  His love can satisfy, 89.
  Of Jesus, 36, 55, 58, 172.
  Of the Shepherd, 100.
Mercy, 215.
Miscellaneous.
  Evils of intemperance, 245.
  I have prayed for thee, 131.
  My Country 'Tis of Thee, 207.
  Over and over, 164.
  Place called Calvary, 183.
  Welcome for me, 135.
  You may have the joy bells, 114.
Missionary, 229, 247.
Obedience, 116, 161.
Peace, 23, 34, 51, 74, 220.
Praise, 3, 4, 53, 130, 196, 208, 210, 239, 246, 256.
Prayer, 31, 45, 91, 189.
Promises, 5, 12, 149, 231.
Redeemed, 177.
Rejoicing, 5, 11, 32, 35, 50, 53, 71, 72, 76, 92, 179, 201, 209.
Rest, 70, 85, 119, 254.
Revival, 210, 241.
Safety, 88, 195.
Salvation, 42, 46.
  An uttermost salvation, 123, 192.
  Hidden riches, 140.
  Send a wave of, 145.
Sowing and reaping, 79, 148, 162.
Sunlight, 18, 22, 80, 81.
Supplication, 15, 24, 243, 263.
  For a wave of salvation, 145.
  For perfect trust, 125.
  For the Holy Spirit, 181.
  Hold Thou my hand, 63.
  Make me a child of Thine, 115.
  Save them to-day, 29.
  Stay my mind on Thee, 133.
Testimony, 9, 49, 98, 139, 234.
  I am saved by faith, 102.
  I was poor as, 47.
  Shall I tell you why, 44.
  What makes the Christian happy, 109.
Warfare, 45, 124, 186, 253.
  Conquerors, 82.
  Go forward, 108, 219.
  Fill up the ranks, 132.
  'Neath the banner, 67.
  Victory, 56, 111, 187.
Work, 60, 79, 132, 156, 162.
  I'll go where, 161.
  Some souls for Jesus, 40, 78.
  Speak a word, 139.
  Why not be a helper, 146.
Worship, 83, 117, 130, 239.

INDEX.

Titles in CAPITALS, First lines in Roman, Choruses in *Italics*.

Abide with me fast 232	COME, BLESSED COM 188	From Greenland's I 229
ABLE AND WILLING. 46	Come, every soul by 165	
A charge to keep... 243	*Come home, come ho* 167	GATHERING SHEAVES 162
A GIFT OF LOVE.... 26	Come sinners, to the 199	Glory be to the Fath 4
ALL IN THY HANDS 38	Come thou fount... 256	GLORIA PATRI...... 4
All hail the power of 238	COME TO JESUS..... 165	GLORY TO HIS NAM 212
All praise to Him w 195	Come thou almighty 208	Go FORWARD...... 108
ALL TO CHRIST I O 205	COME TO THE FOUNT 143	God calling yet..... 214
All to Jesus I surren 224	*Come unto me all ye* 10	God will take care o 150
ALL THE DAY LONG 10	Come ye disconsolat 230	Guide me, O thou... 259
Along the way of li 41	Come ye, poor wand 20	Grace divine since t 23
Am I a soldier of th 253	Come ye, sinners... 258	
And can I yet delay. 244	Comforter, in my he 97	HALLELUJAH, let the 130
AN UTTERMOST SALV 123	*Coming home, comi* 157	*Hallelujah, he has o* 72
Are You in the Inner 152	*Coming home, the w* 179	*Hallelujah, Thine th* 210
Are You Ready, Are 95	CORONATION DAY.... 95	HAPPY DAY........ 32
Are thy days full oft 93	CONQUERORS THROU. 82	*Happy day, happy d* 209
Arouse ye men of w 108	Contrite I kneel to t 24	Hark, the trump of 60
ASHAMED OF JESUS. 134	CROWN HIM, KING. 117	Have you heard the 152
As the two disciples 128		Have we learned the 56
A WAVE OF SALVATIO 145	DEAR TO THE HEART 100	HAVE YOU FOUND TH 33
Away to the Battlefi 186	DEEPER YET........ 222	HEAVEN IS MY HOM 202
A wondrous mine of 140	Do NOT CHASE AWA 80	HEAVENLY SUNLIGH 81
	Does your heart gro 84	HE CAME TO SAVE M 201
BAPTIZED WITH THE 169	Down at the cross... 212	HE'LL NEVER FORSAK 137
BEARING THE BANNE 156	Do you seek a land 169	HE KNOWS IT ALL. 103
BE GALLANT IN THE 67		HE ROLLED THE SEA 217
BEHOLD THE SAVIOUR 62	ENTIRE CONSECRATIO 221	HEREAFTER 19
Beloved, now are we 180	EVENTIDE 232	*Here the Blessed Sa* 106
BE STILL AND KNOW 197	Every day my heart 92	HE SAVES ME....... 178
Beyond the winter's 6	*Every step my Savio* 141	HE SHIELDS FROM T 195
BLESSED BE THE NAM 196	EVERY WORD I BELI 149	HE'S THE ONE...... 68
BLESSED COMMUNION 64	Eye hath not seen.. 140	He was not willing t 46
Blessed peace, O wo 51		He will mention the 35
Blest promise of Jes 70	FAITH, HOPE AND LO 142	He will hear me wh 170
Blest be the tie that 242	Far away in the dep 34	HIDDEN RICHES..... 140
BRING SOME ONE TO 40	Fear not, I am with 52	HIDING FROM THE S 88
Burdened with a loa 97	FILL UP THE RANKS 132	*Hid behind the Cro* 182
But O, the joy when 190	FLOWING EVER...... 87	*His power can make* 17
BY AND BY......... 93	*Flowing for me*..... 66	HIS WAY WITH TH 17
By and by I shall see 37	FOLLOW ALL THE WA 194	HIS LOVE CAN SATI. 89
By and by we will re 90	FOLLOW ME......... 122	Hold thou my hand 63
	Forever here my rest 254	HIS PRESENCE ABID 70
Calvary's fountain.. 66	*For like a royal Kin* 123	Holy Ghost with lig 216
Calling, Calling..... 118	For the Lord God is 12	Holy spirit, faithful 211
Calmly leaning on m 220	For the people of G 85	*Hosanna, hosanna...* 5
Can it be, O can it be 163	FOR YOU AND FOR ME 167	*How beautiful to wa* 200
Chase them not awa 80	*Forward, forward to* 108	How hopeless was t 42
CHRIST IS ALL...... 96	Forward to Canaan's 156	How sweet the name 255
CHRIST IS SUFFICIEN 144	*Free, free pardoned* 9	HE SAVES ME....... 178
COME AS YOU ARE.. 20	From all that dwell 246	I AM SAVED BY FAIT 102

222

I entered once a ho	96	Jesus is lovingly call	73	Never Leave Thee.	101
I ask, O Lord, that t	125	*Jesus, Jesus, how I*	219	*No friend like Jesus*	41
I believe it, every	43	Jesus' Love has M	92	No longer from Jesu	66
If you ask me why	149	Jesus, lover of my so	228	*Now I lay me down*	91
If you are tired of t	166	Jesus Only........	8	Not by my trying, no	98
I have found a great	113	*Jesus paid it all.....*	205	Nothing But the B	204
I have a friend, a pre	58	Jesus Saves Me, Jes	113	Nothing earthly ince	8
I had heard the Gos	154	Jesus shall reign wh	247	Now the day is over	198
I have found a place	182	Jesus Sweetly Save	154		
I Have Prayed for	131	Jesus the Saviour so	118	O blessed token of t	51
I have heard of a be	168	*Joy bells, ringing in*	114	O Blessed Hope....	180
I have heard my Sav	194	Just as I am without	237	O'er the ocean of ti	86
I Have the Witnes	98	*Just now your doubt*	166	O for a faith that ca	142
I hear the Saviour sa	205			O for a faith that wi	252
I'll Awaken in th	173	Keep on Praying..	45	O for a heart to prai	251
I'll be There......	203	Kind is the heart of	59	O for a thousand..	239
I'll go where You	161			O happy day that fix	209
I'll Live and Ne'er	190	Lead Me, Saviour..	174	O heart bereaved an	103
I'll be present when	16	Leaning on the Cr	106	O How He Loves M	58
I'll love him till the	134	Leaning on the E	171	*O it is good to be th*	64
I'm but a stranger..	202	Let Jesus Come Int	166	O, Jesus, thou art st	227
I'm never alone in s	99	Let the Holy Ghos	84	*O let the language o*	125
I Must Tell Jesus	7	Let the Saviour in.	176	O let us rejoice in th	104
I'm So Glad.......	201	Let us look up to Jc	167	O, Lord, send a wav	145
In a Little While	107	Let us sing a song t	107	O, Lord, show thy m	29
I Never can forget	189	List! 'tis Jesus' Vo	136	On a lone, lone, hill	55
I Never Will Leav	21	Living in the Sun	22	Once a troubled mot	31
In heaven the skies	61	Looking for Me....	138	Once far from my J	49
In seasons that come	135	Looking this Way	75	One Thing I Know	184
In the blood from th	222	Lord carest thou not	48	Only a Little Pray	31
In the Cross of Chr	240	*Lord help me.......*	31	On Lone Calvary.	55
In the morning, bles	173	Lord I am thine en	249	O mourner in Zion.	231
In heavenly love abi	110	Lord, I'm Coming H	157	O now I see the crim	236
In the land where J	19	Lost But Not Fors	234	On the cross my Sa	172
In the riven rock..	88	Love, Love.........	112	On the good old roa	50
In thy hands, O Jes	43			On to Victory.....	187
Is there any one ca	68	Make Me a Child o	115	Onward like a migh	87
I Shall be no Stra	185	My blessed redeeme	65	Open the Windows	18
I Shall be Like...	153	My Companion Un	121	Open Wide the Gat	11
I Shall See My De	37	My country, 'tis of t	207	O, sinner, your Savi	136
I Surrender All...	224	My days are gliding	218	O some day I'll sor	28
Into His Marvello	73	My faith looks up to	216	*O spirit of love desc*	181
It is Jesus, the Lord	121	My Grace is Suffi	30	O spread the tidings	193
It may not be o'er th	161	My Jesus I love thee	213	*O summer land.....*	6
I was a slave in the	9	My Jesus, loving Je	129	O Sweet Rest.....	85
I was lost but not fo	234	My life is full of sun	72	*O there is a city, a*	160
I am not skilled to u	191	My Little Evening	91	O the joyous greetin	13
I Was Poor as the	4	My Mother's Pray	189	O troubled heart no l	89
I Want to Know M	147	Mourn for the thous	245	O, thou bleeding, la	183
I will fail thee never	137	My Saviour (He wi	170	O 'Twas Love......	172
I Will Go, I Canno	163	My Saviour (I am n	191	*Out in desert they w*	100
I will trust him all	141	My Sins Are all T	35	O What a Wonder	65
I've Been Redeemed	177	My sins are forgiven	144	Over and Over.....	164
I've wandered far a	157			Over the river, faces	75
		Nearer, Still Near	223	O ye thirsty ones tha	155
Jesus and shall it ev	250	Nearer the Cross..	151		
Jesus Bears my Bu	94	Nearer, my God, to	150	Pardoned and Free	9
Jesus Christ my Par	11	Nearer the Shore.	86	Passeth Understan	51
Jesus Has Lifted t	53	Near, near to my Sa	64	Peace is Mine.....	23
Jesus, I my Cross h	257	'Neath his banner br	67	*Peace, Peace, Wonder*	34
Jesus is Near......	99	Never Alone........	52	Perfect Trust in T	125

223

PLACE CALLED CALVA 183	THE HEAVENLY SU 6	WAITING FOR THE KI 126
Praise the Lord..... 50	The judgment day is 57	Wandering in the wi 138
PROMISES OF JESUS. 5	THE INNER CIRCLE.. 152	WALK IN THE LIGHT 27
	THE LIGHT OF GOD'S 158	Walking in sunlight 81
Rejoice, rejoice with 179	THE LIVING WATERS 72	WALKING WITH THE 110
Rest, sweet rest..... 70	THE LORD IS MY LIG 71	*Was ever known suc* 55
Revive thy work, O 241	THE MASTER'S ON B 48	*Wash me in the Sav* 22
REVIVE US AGAIN.. 210	The palace of God's 74	*We are nearing the* 86
RINGING SWEETLY ON 127	The Saviour's arms. 195	We are willing work 79
Rock of Ages...... 226	The Seer came back 30	We are waiting for t 126
Rouse ye for service 124	THE SAVIOUR'S CALL 118	*We hear the angels* 127
	The shepherd is cros 77	*We'll sing the praise* 83
Salvation full, salva 199	THE SHINING SHORE 218	WELCOME FOR ME... 135
Satan hath desired t 131	THE SINNER'S FRIE 129	We praise Thee, O 210
SAVED THROUGH JES 16	The trusting heart to 53	*We will crown him* 117
SAVED TO THE UTTER 192	THE UNSEEN COUNT 25	We will journey ho 76
SAVE ME JUST NOW 24	THE WANDERERS AR 179	What a fellowship, 171
SAVE THEM TO-DAY 29	The world was all I 44	What a friend we ha 225
Saviour, lead me lest 174	There are foes that 187	WHAT ARE YOU SOW 148
SAVIOUR WALK WIT 128	There are the songs 130	What can wash awa 204
SEEKING TO SAVE.. 77	There are times whe 173	WHAT MAKES THE 109
Send Lord a wave of 145	There's a beautiful d 158	Whatever sorrows g 101
SHALL I TELL YOU 44	There's a form walk 121	*Whene'er I think of* 189
Since Christ hath re 94	There is a fountain 177	WHEN HE COMES A 13
Since I heard my ble 106	There is a land of p 203	When I shall reach 153
SINGING ALL THE W 76	There is a sacred me 91	When I survey the 248
Singing I go along 53	There's a happy ho 37	When Israel out of b 217
SINGING ON THE W 50	THERE'S A LIGHTON 90	When Jesus laid his 201
Sing of the wonder 36	There's a wideness.. 215	WHEN THE LIGHT B 28
Softly and tenderly 167	There's many a soul 146	When the morning l 133
Soldier is the battle 45	THERE'S NO FRIEND. 41	When the pearly ga 185
SOME DAY I'M GOIN 168	THERE IS POWER IN 69	WHEN THE ROLL IS 159
SOME SWEET DAY.. 39	There's plenty in our 123	When the shadows o 14
Some time in hours 120	There's strength for 12	When the trumpet o 159
Some time, some da 119	*Then forward still 't* 217	When we walk with 116
Some day my earthl 190	This the promise Go 111	*Where he leads me I* 194
Some time we'll stan 16	THE SOME DAY BY 14	WHO IS THIS?...... 54
SOULS FOR JESUS... 78	Though in this worl 21	Whom shall I meet 25
SPEAK A WORD..... 139	Though a sinner sic 234	WHOSOEVER WILL M 155
SPEAK TO MY SOUL 15	*Thou wilt keep him* 74	Who will testify for 139
STAY MY MIND ON 133	*They are all taken aw* 35	WHY NOT BE A HEL 146
STEP OUT ON THE P 231	THY HOLY SPIRIT L 181	*Why will ye wander* 155
Stepping in the Li 200	'TIS A GREAT SALVA 42	*Will you be baptized* 169
STILL SWEETER EVER 175	'Tis the Saviour who 176	WINNING ITS WAY. 104
STRENGTH FOR MY D 12	'Tis so sweet to trus 219	With mansions of fai 160
Sun of my soul..... 235	*'Tis that he knows t* 109	Wonderful love sent 112
SWEET LAND OF BLI 120	To HIM BE GLORY.. 130	WONDERFUL LOVE OF 36
SWEET SUMMER LAN 61	To Jesus every day 175	WONDERFUL PEACE.. 34
	TO THE WORK...... 60	*Wonderful place call* 183
Take my life and let 233	To redeem my life f 26	WORKING FOR THE M 79
Take my life and let 45	TRUST AND OBEY.... 116	Work in the harvest 162
THAT GREAT DAY O 57	Trying to walk in th 200	Would you be free f 69
THE ARROW OF LOV 49		Would you live for 17
THE BEAUTIFUL CIT 160	UPHELD BY THE POW 105	
Thy cleansing strea 236	UP WITH THE BANN 124	*Yes, a satisfying*.... 170
THE COMFORTER HA 193		Yes, hereafter we sh 19
The dear loving Sav 178	VICTORY ALL THE W 56	*Yes, since my Savio* 92
THE GOSPEL FEAST. 199	VICTORY ALL THE TI 111	*Yes, there's one*.... 68
THE GRANDEST SONG 83	*Victory, Victory al* 56	YOU MAY HAVE THE 114
The half cannot be f 175	Volunteers are want 186	*Your sins he will fo* 62
THE HEAVEN SIDE.. 182	VOLUNTEERS TO THE 186	

224

www.ingramcontent.com/pod-product-compliance
Lightning Source LLC
Chambersburg PA
CBHW022016220426
43663CB00007B/1099